CHRIST
WHO IS ABOVE
ALL THINGS

By Rev. O.K. Adeagbo

CHRIST WHO IS ABOVE ALL THINGS
PUBLISHED by Rev.OK. ADEAGBO
1 Elm Tree Court, Fairlawn Charlton
London SE7 7DP
Email Revadeagbo@aol.com

Scripture quotations are from King James Version:

Re-printed and bound in the United Kingdom, by WATKISS Studios limited
Biggleswade, Bedfordshire SG18 9ST

OK Adeagbo 2000:
Re-published 2000, @O.K ADEAGBO 2000

ISBN_ 0 9539500 0 X _____

DEDICATION

THE CHRIST WHO IS ABOVE ALL

This book is dedicated to the Glory of Jesus Christ, the Son of the ever living God who brought us up also out of an horrible pit, out of the miry clay, Psalm 40:2, and set our feet upon a rock 1 Cor 10:4; who hath delivered us from the power of darkness, and has translated us into the kingdom of His dear son. In whom we have redemption through his blood, even the forgiveness of sin of which mine were many.

Christ Jesus, who is the image of the invisible God, the first-born of every creature Colossians 1:13-15. I say Praise be to His Holy name, of He that was, He that is, and He that is alive for evermore.

God did so many good things, which the Bible could not contain, indeed which the whole world could not contain if everyone were to write a book on what He did John 21:25 for He is surely above all.

I will continue to praise God who blessed me with a very loving wife who is comfortable to be with, generous to all she meets, living up to her name "Comfort". She is a great gift of God to me.

The book could not be completed without the help of my children who read and commented on the book. I say thanks and God bless you all.

To all others who have contributed to this book in no small way, I say the Lord Himself shall reward you - Amen.

The book is written with a clear mind, and clear conscience given by the Holy Spirit of God. We are all the works of God's hand. He is our father. He is our potter, and we are the clay Isaiah 64:8.

The book is written for everyone to read and gain a clear and unbiased view of who Jesus Christ, the Son of God is, what He did, what He is now doing, and what He shall do in the future.

As you read on, I pray that you will be blessed, and that all your needs, including salvation, be supplied by God according to His riches in glory by Christ Jesus Phil 4:19 (Amen). It is written that ye may be a child of your father which is in heaven, i.e. God Almighty, not your deceased earthly father, i.e. He that makes the sun to rise on the evil and on the good, and sends rain on the just and on the unjust Mt 5:45.

for your money, but rather for your salvation". In my old religion I had felt 'saved' as a big contributor to the mosque building fund, yet here I was being told I was not saved. I later came to understand that without Christ in my life, I was like a filthy rag, Isa. 64: 6-7.

They kept on coming to our house as though they had no other place to go. They would pray, sing and a talk about Jesus Christ. Even though I had cars, they would send the church bus with two men to collect us to make sure we came. There is nothing I could pay these men for their persistence, and for seeing that I became BORN AGAIN. Praise God, that the Redeemed Christian Church of God chose to stand by me at the time.

I then began reading the Bible trying to find a place where Jesus had said that a man would come after him to save the world. Having read the bible from cover to cover over 10 times, I haven't found it.

What did I find instead? I found the Comforter who is the Holy Spirit, who will abide with the believers forever. Even the spirit of truth whom the world cannot receive because it sees Him not, neither knows him; but the Christians (ye) know Him; for He dwelleth with you, and shall be in you John 14:16-17. By all accounts, this is not a physical man who is mortal, but the immortal Spirit of God.

My wife and I were invited to join the church workers, which meant starting church at 6.00am on Sundays to go and evangelise, attend church meetings, and prepare the church.

Having worked for a while as a Sunday School Teacher, then as an Assistant Pastor I was eventually offered the opportunity to go and pastor a church in a remote village in Ibadan which two other Pastors had turned down.

To God's glory, I was given a very hardworking man as an assistant. On the first day in the village, we met a man who said that he is a Muslim, and warned us about the big guns in the village who would make sure we left the village just like previous churches that had tried to come in and stay.

I remembered God's encouraging words "Go son", from the day I came to know him three years previously.

I asked the man if there were any Christians left in the area, and he told me there were some 'white garment' Christians about the place.

Within a month of us being in the area, the church grew by six members, so there were 8 of us who sang praises to God at the top of our voices, jumping and dancing in the Lord - our racket being heard up to a quarter of a mile away.

Small children came to stand outside the church, dancing with us while their parents were at home. We would then visit their homes, and invite their parents. Many obliged, whilst others said 'they would rather die than join us'.

One day, the Lord told me to organise a House fellowship which I did. During one session, five people came up for prayers, and as I prayed for the one closest to me she began shaking. I left her and prayed for the others, not knowing what I was about to witness.

As soon as I went back to her and declared 'In the Name of Jesus', the woman, a Muslim known as Silifat, went down flat on her back, giving me quite a fright. After a while, she began drumming her tummy so hard that everyone ran out except my assistant and the woman's uncle. I laid my hand on her tummy and she began banging her chest until she vomited some black stuff like grass. She yelled 'I vomit it out' and then got to her feet. Her uncle attested that she had been given a potion over 22 years ago, and had been in an unstable mental state since then.

The following Sunday, the church grew by about seventeen new 'curious' members, including Muslims who had come to see what was going on.

In the three years I remained in the village, people were coming from over sixty kilometres away on our Deliverance Days, to partake in God's plan to set the captives free.

God's word says that "At His name, every knee shall bow, of things in heaven, and things in earth, and things under the earth', and that 'every tongue shall confess that Jesus Christ is Lord to the glory of God the Father" Phil. 2:10-11. God shall never cease the business of healing, deliverance, miracles, signs and wonders. Praise be to His Holy name. Amen.

CHRIST ABOVE ALL GOSPEL CHURCH IS BORN

As the Lord was working in my old church, we arranged monthly deliverance services which, at the end, brought people from far and near as God performed miracle upon miracle.

Moreso, God was touching Muslims and Christians alike in the church, God being no respecter of persons Acts 10:34. The man who said the church would not last a month, not only saw the church grow in number, but also saw his two children become members.

It was during a deliverance service that a Pastor and her entourage from a Cherubim and Seraphim church came to see what we were about. The Lord touched her, and she was on the floor for an hour and a half. When she came to, I told her that I did not die on the Calvary cross, the Cherubims and Seraphims did not die on the cross, but rather that Jesus Christ had died on the cross.

She said that what she had seen that day was enough to convince her to accept the Gospel. She said she didn't want to join Redeemed, that she wanted to change her church name and invited me to Pastor the church and tell them the true Gospel of Jesus Christ. The name 'Christ above all' came to me, and God's church is still thriving.

IN THE BEGINNING WAS THE WORD-JOHN 1: 1-18

In the beginning was the Word, and the Word was with God, inseparable from God John 10:30.

Just as the word you speak cannot be separated from you the speaker, so also Jesus Christ who said unto Jesus "If God were your Father, you would love me: for I proceeded forth and came from God; neither came I of myself just as the word we speak goes out according to our will as we send it, so also God sent His word, John 8:42, to create all things that are in heaven, and that are in earth; visible or invisible, whether they be thrones, or dominions, or principalities, or powers; all things were created by him and for him. He is before all things, and by him all things exist. He is the Head of the body, the Church; who is the beginning, the first born from the dead, that in all things he might have the pre-eminence.

He was before all things, and just as we are commended to give honour to our father and our mother, that our days may be long upon the land which the Lord our God gives us Exo 20:12, so also must we honour Jesus Christ the Lord who said that many people do not give him pre-eminence in their lives. But it is an honour with their lips, alas! But their heart is far from the Word of God. Matt 15:8.

In Him was life, and the life was the light of men that shined through the stronghold of the kingdom of darkness, and great is the power of light, that darkness cannot swallow the light of God. Wherever the light shines the darkness flees. Christ is the true light of God which lights every man that comes into the world. He said that as long as he is in the world, He is the light of the world John 9:5. He had opened a blind man's eyes. Who can then give light to a blind like Jesus. He that planted the ear, shall he not hear? He that formed the eye, shall he not see? Psalm 94:9 The hearing ear, and the seeing eye, the Lord Jesus hath made even both of them Prov. 20:12.

John the Baptist said that he came for a witness of the light, which is the Word of God, that men through him might believe that there is God, that man needs salvation, that Jesus Christ is the Saviour of all men, specially of those that believe 1 Tim 4:10. John continued his testimony that He was in the world, and the world was made by him, and the world knew him not. He came into his own, and his own received him not, though it was necessary that the Word of God should first have been spoken to them, but seeing they put it from them, and judged themselves unworthy of everlasting life, it came to the Gentiles. Acts 13:46.

But as many as received the Word of God, that came to the world, to them gave he power to become the sons of God, even to them that believe on his name, those who have not received the spirit of bondage again to fear; those who have received the spirit of adoption, whereby they cry Abba Father. Those who their spirit itself bear witness that they are the children of God, those who are ready to suffer with Jesus Christ, that they may also be glorified together as Sons of God. Rom18:15-17.

The Word was made flesh, and dwells among us. With God nothing shall be impossible Lk 1:37, and we beheld his glory, the glory as of the only begotten of the Father confirmed by Jesus Christ, after putting on the flesh that God so loved the world that he gave his only begotten son that whosoever believes in him should not perish, but have everlasting life. John 3:16.

In him, the fullness of the time was come. God sent his son, made of a woman, made under the law.

John the Baptist, a respected prophet as Yah-Yah in Islam bore witness of Jesus and cried, saying "This was he of whom I spoke", He that comes after me is preferred before me; for he was before me, preached saying "There comes one mightier than I after me, the latches of whose shoes I am not worthy to stoop down and unloose. Who can bend down to unloose God's shoes? God is covered by fire, for He is the Consuming Fire.

He went further to say "Indeed, I have baptised you with water, but Jesus Christ shall baptise you with the Holy Ghost Mark 1:7-8.

John did not keep silent as he said "No man has seen God at any time for He is invisible" 1 Tim 1:17; the only begotten son, which is in the bosom of the Father, he hath declared him.

The Jews challenged John, asking why he should baptise at all. He admitted "I am not the Christ". Are you E-li-as? They believed in the resurrection, and did see the saints that came out when Christ resurrected (see Resurrection of Jesus). John said, I am not, Art thou the prophet, i.e. Christ whom Israel expected? I tell you one thing, that had he said he was, they would have been so glad to receive him; water baptism is simple, but baptism with the Holy Ghost and fire which burns is another thing. No, they wouldn't like that, as proved in the chapter on 'Battleground'.

Who are you, that we may give an account to them that sent us? What say you of yourself? They were waiting for an answer.

He said, I am the voice of one crying in the wilderness, I came to make straight the way of the Lord, as said the prophet, E-Sai-as, saying "Prepare ye the way of the Lord, make straight in the desert a highway for our God".

Every valley shall be exalted, and every mountain and hill shall be made low, and the crooked shall be made straight, and the rough places plain.

And the glory of the Lord shall be revealed, and all flesh shall see it together for the mouth of the Lord hath spoken it Isa 40:3-5.

The next day, John saw Jesus coming to him, and said "Behold the Lamb of God, which takes away the sin of the world", i.e. the Word of God, "that put on flesh to become man Jesus, the Lamb of God".

"Look at him properly, he is after me, and preferred before me for he was before me. I knew him not, but that he should be made known to Israel, therefore am I come baptising with water. I am not going beyond my boundary, I saw the spirit descending from heaven like a dove, and it abode upon him, and I knew him not; but he that sent me to baptise with water, the same said unto me, upon whom thou shall see the spirit descending, and remaining not as on Elijah, Elisha and the rest on whose head the spirit descended and departed after a particular undertaking was fulfilled, the same is he which baptises with the Holy Ghost, and if you all don't mind and are not offended in who I am talking about, I saw, and bare record of what you hate to hear that this is the Son of God" John 1:1-36.

Now, let us reason together that He is older than anybody that had come, and will come to this world, for he is the Ancient of Days, who did sit on the thrones, whose garment was white as snow, and the hair of his head was like pure wool; whose throne was like the fiery flame, and his wheels as burning fire Daniel 7:9.

If by strength, the Word of God is the power of God that is above human instruments, but Word spoken, which is sharper than a two edged sword. It is written "For the Word of God is quick, and powerful, and sharper than (any human sword) a two edged sword, piercing even to the dividing asunder of soul and spirit, and of the joints and marrow, and is a discerner of the thoughts (omniscient) and intents of the heart Heb 4:12.

I submit to you today that the Word of God used by you as a believer will accomplish that to which you direct it for God is not a man that he should lie, neither the son of man that he should repent. "Hath he said it and shall he not do it, or hath he spoken it, and shall he not make it good?" Numbers 23:19.

A couple recently brought their baby for dedication in church. They came with friends, and by the end of the service it was raining very heavily outside. This reminded me of a situation when I was a pastor in Nigeria where we had a program scheduled for which the rain was threatening to spoil the day.

A man came up to me, apparently very happy to see the dark skies looming. He asked me if we were still going to hold the service. I took my bible in my hand, opened it, and said "Rain, in the name of Jesus, who is above you! Stay where you are and don't come out until after our program".

People came in their droves, many were saved and everyone went home dry. The rain came down in torrents the next day, destroying many huts and homes, but the man who had asked if the service was still to hold came up to me and exclaimed "It worked! It worked". I told him my word didn't work, but God's word always works.

I went out during this more recent dedication in church and applied God's same word to the rain, and it worked yet again.

I guess those who saw me outside would say "Isn't this going too far", but it wasn't crazy, neither was I going too far. Consider this, "Then spoke Joshua to the Lord in the day when the Lord delivered up the Amorites before the children of Israel, and he said in the sight of Israel, Sun, stand thou still upon Gibeon; and thou Moon in the valley of Aj-a-lon." And the sun stood still, and the moon stayed until the people had avenged themselves upon their enemies. Joshua 10:12-13.

God's word will always work. If it worked to create the heavens and the earth, it will work at any time, any place, and used by any man who believes in the Word of God which is Jesus Christ.

HE SENT HIS WORD - PSALM 107:20

Whenever we send someone on an errand, we give them all the necessary equipment to accomplish what we send them to do.

We are happy to provide transport money, or vehicles to take the person to the destination, and anything else necessary for the person to achieve the objectives we have set them. God armed His Word, Jesus Christ John 1:1 fully, with the Holy Ghost and with power over everything, that he went about doing good. Healing all that were oppressed of the devil, for God was with him Acts 10:38.

He sent his word to show us who He is, what He is like, that he is a good God, to let us know that he is unlike the idols that are dumb and static in a place. That he wishes above all things that we may prosper on this earth, and be in health, even as our souls prosper 3 John 2.

No one can make these three things happen by themselves. But everything is possible by the Lord, God who makes one to prosper 2 Chro 26:5 whose blessing makes rich and adds no sorrow with it Prov. 10:22. "The prosperity of fools shall destroy them, says he, who sent his Word" Prov. 1:32. He said that you should not be envious of them when you see them prosper and increase in riches Psalm 73:3:12. God's Word is true and sure. He says that he wishes above all things that you may prosper. He meant what he said, and with Christ on your side, you will prosper as he wished for you.

Now he said that he wishes above all things that you be in health. He has said it, and it shall be so. "If you will diligently hearken to the voice of the Lord your God, and will do that which is right in his sight, and will give ear to his commandments, and keep all his statutes, I will put none of these diseases, poverty, lacks, and wants, high blood pressure, asthma, AIDS, cancer, blindness and arthritis upon thee, which I have brought upon the Egyptians; for I am the Lord that healeth thee Exo. 15:26.

He said that he wishes above all things that even your soul prospers, so that he may redeem your soul that you shall not be desolate Psalm 34:22.

All things that are needed to live a good life could not be attained by natural means. God had to do something. He himself had to take care of it all, and he therefore sent his Word, and healed them of poverty, lack, and wants, and all sorts of sickness, and brought us to himself through his son who took care of all our infirmities on the Calvary Cross, body, soul and spirit taken care off. It remains for every one to look unto him and believe, and whoever does shall never be put to shame. Romans 9:33.

The Word that God sent put on flesh to become man, Jesus the Son of God upon whom the Spirit of the Lord God is rested and anointed to preach good tidings, who was sent to bind up the broken-hearted, to proclaim liberty (freedom) to the captives in physical, material, and spiritual bondage, and to deliver all under spiritual wickedness in high places and bring them to God Almighty.

It is quite surprising to see one supposed uncircumcised soldier to know that God sent His word to heal. Jesus entered into Capernaum, then this Roman Centurion came in begging, and saying "Lord, I do recognise who you are, that God is with you, I know that the authority is yours, see my servant who I love lies at home sick of the palsy, and he is grievously tormented. I am very concerned, as you can see, I have invited the doctors from Rome after the military doctors have failed, and they too could do nothing. I do know one thing that neither palsy nor anything is beyond your power to heal. I do perceive that God sent you as his Word to heal, here am I at your mercy for you are compassionate."

Jesus said to him, "I will come and heal him, since you know that with God nothing shall be impossible, and that I can. Let us go to your place".

The Centurion could discern the power in the Word spoken by Jesus Christ. He was thinking also of the time lag between where they were and his house. He said, "please Master, I am not worthy that you should come under my roof, but SPEAK THE WORD only, speak that authoritative and commanding word, and my servant , I am 100 percent sure, shall be healed", for God has sent His word to heal and deliver us from our destructions Psm 107:20.

"Lord, you know that I am a man under authority, having soldiers under me, and I say to this man, Go, and he goes; and to another come, and he comes. I have no doubt that all power is in your hand, just speak the word of healing now, my Lord."

The Bible says that when Jesus heart this Centurion's words, which were not words of flattery, but a recognition of Christ's authority and who Jesus is, he was marvelled that the Centurion passed the test of recognition where the Jews failed, then he said to them that followed him "Verily, I say unto you, I have not found so great faith, no not in Israel."

And I say unto you, that many shall come from the east and the west, and shall sit down with Abraham and Isaac, and Jacob in the kingdom of heaven; Gentiles will accept the salvation of God in faith as you all today see this Centurion. But the children of the kingdom who should know better, but did not, shall be cast out into outer darkness; there shall be weeping and gnashing of teeth.

And Jesus said unto the Centurion who recognised that truly Christ is above all things "Go thy way because you discern who I am, and believe what you believe, so be it done unto thee. AND HIS SERVANT WAS HEALED IN THE SELF-SAME HOUR. Remember that God sent his Word, and his Word heals us Ps. 107:20."

The Word is packed with the power of God, and be it known to you today that nothing can hinder the Word of God, even Satan, the father of all demons tried to exchange words with the Word of God, Satan failed. As the Spirit led Jesus into the wilderness to be tempted of the devil after forty days and forty nights fasting, he was obviously hungered. Who wouldn't be?

Since Satan had managed to tempt Adam and Eve with food and succeeded, bringing humanity into sin and destruction, he tried a fast one on the Lord of Glory and he failed.

"If thou be the Son of God, itself an acknowledgement that Christ is the Son of God (hallelujah) command (he knew that Christ has the authority) that these stones be made bread". Obey me, the devil was saying. He forgot that he was not speaking to a human being, but to his maker.

The Word that healeth came out "It is written", signed, sealed and delivered by

God, that "Man shall not live by bread alone, but by every word that proceeds out of the mouth of God" Mt 8:3.

The devil does not leave any one alone. He goes for a while, only to come back again; be prepared, be alert, be armed with the Word of God.

Then the devil took Jesus into the holy city and set him on a pinnacle of the temple, and said to him "If thou be the Son of God (he wanted to get Jesus to obey him by proving what he challenged) cast yourself down for it is written He shall give his angels charge concerning thee; and in their hands they shall bear thee up, lest at any time thou dash thy foot against a stone" Psalm 91:12. Here was Satan quoting the scripture. You must remain one step ahead of him, and that means having Jesus Christ in your life. He is the one above Satan's tricks, no one else but Jesus.

Christ said unto him "It is written again, thou shalt not tempt the Lord thy God" Dt. 6:16. The devil will come and come again, be at alert, the Bible says "Be sober, be vigilant, because your adversary the devil as a roaring lion (not truly a lion, Christ is the Lion of Judah Rev. 5:5) walking about, seeking whom he may devour 1 Peter 5:8.

The devil taketh him up into an exceeding high mountain, and sheweth him all the kingdoms of the world, and the glory of them, and said unto him "all these things will I give you (things which did not belong to him; but the earth is the Lord's and the fullness thereof, the world and they that dwell therein Psalm 24:1). Satan demanded an obeisance, i.e. that Jesus fall down to worship him. Christ commanded him "Get thee hence behind me Satan, for it is written Thou shalt worship the Lord thy God, and him only shalt thou serve" Mt 4:1-11.

As Jesus resisted the devil, he ran away. Behold, angels came and ministered to Jesus.

You have to give time for the Word of God, so that you may be able to face the fiery darts of the devil who, from time to time, will be coming back to see whether you are asleep or awake as to the Word of Life, which is the Word of God. Do not allow him to catch you unawares, for if he does, he will make sure he torments you, and there is no escape.

ARREST MY WORD

There was a criminal caught red-handed, taken to court. His lawyer tried to quote laws upon laws to get him free. The lawyer's hope was rising. In 000 versus 0001, the lawyer raised an objection to the prosecutor, the judge came in to say "objection overruled", which is normal if the judge feels that what has been said is unnecessary or irrelevant to the case.

There was nothing that the whole court could do than to burst into laughter when the criminal said to the judge "Why is the objection overruled". He then launched an abusive tirade at the judge, and everyone stopped laughing as the man was arraigned before the court, and charged for contempt of court.

The criminal stopped talking, and his lawyer tried to patch up the unpatchable. "Your Honour, don't think I am mentally deranged. I am not. I know all I am going to tell you now, hold me not accountable; hold my word but not me, your Honour. I know what is in your mind, that something must be wrong with me, but I do know that twenty-five multiplied by itself is six hundred and twenty five, and if it pleases you, your Honour, you can give me another mental arithmetic.

Then the judge asked "where is your word to be prosecuted?" As far as I am concerned, as far as the court is concerned, unless you produce your word in physical form , you standing there in the dock are accountable for your actions whether in deeds, words or thought put into action. He said to the criminal, there is no difference between you and whatever words you speak. He thus gave the criminal six months for contempt of court.

Christ is the same to God, as that man's word was to him. That's why he said he and his father are one John 10:30. He is the Word that was sent to loose the bands of wickedness, to undo the heavy burdens, and to let he oppressed go free, and he broke every yoke; he fed the hungry and he clothed the naked.

Unless you can separate even the Word, you speak from yourself and say it is not you, then you can't separate Jesus Christ from God. They are one. When you know that he is the Word of God, make use of the opportunity given to you. The Word is inviting you now. "Come unto me all ye that labour and are heavy laden, and I will give you rest from all that you think is impossible to achieve in your life.

Take my yoke upon you, try my way, and learn of me. Follow my guide, for I am meek and lowly, willing to meet your needs, that your soul shall be at rest; and peace will take control of the turmoil of your life. For my yoke is not like those that are not God-given, for I do not over-burden anyone that comes to me. I, on the other hand, will relieve you of your burdens for I am a problem solver. I will not put you in a position of difficulty, and I will still the tempest in your life for you Mt 11: 28-30.

THE TEMPEST STILLED

There is nothing that the word sent cannot control. The Word can reduce mountains to rubble. He could stay the sun and moon where they are. He is also the controller of the oceans, and the seas are under his domain. He controls where no one else can ask him what he is doing; there is none comparable to him. He is Lord over all situations, higher than the heavens and the earth. He is worthy to praise, Glory and honour are his and his alone. Hallelujah.

One evening, he told the disciples "Let us pass over unto the other side". After sending away the multitude they took him even as he was in the ship. There was also with him other little ships, all unaware of what was in front. However, Christ the omniscient knew .

There was a great storm of wind; greater than the present storm of your life, greater than disappointments you are now encountering, greater than family headache, lack, or anything you may ever imagine. The storm, with mighty waves beat into the ship just as you are tossed here and there by your worries and concerns which are now threatening to overcome you. Your heart is beating as you say "who can you run to?"

It seems that heaven and earth are breaking up. What can you do? I say nothing, for all you need to do is trust in the Lord with all thine heart; and lean not unto thine own understanding Prov. 3:5; and he will rescue you.

He was in the hinder part of the ship, just as he is looking and waiting for what you will do if you are faithful or faithless. He was asleep on a pillow; the angels of God encampeth round about him, he can never be afraid. They woke him up as they were terrified of sinking, forgetting the word of the person in the ship that says "We shall not die but live and declare the works of the Lord" Psalm 118:17, who happily was sailing with them.

"Master, carest thou not that we perish", they asked him. He answered "Yes, I care, but do not be afraid". I have told you to "cast all your care upon me" for, in all things "I care for you". 1 Peter 5:7.

Then he arose, and rebuked the wind with his word, and said unto the sea "listen to your maker who formed thee - Peace be still". Today, Christ says all the troubles of your life be gone, and the peace of God which passes all understanding flow into your life. Amen.

The Bible says that those disciples who had seen miracles upon miracles before, feared exceedingly that this is not the work of man, but God himself, as the wind ceased and there was a great calm by him who rules the raging of the sea; when the waves thereof arise, he stillest them Ps. 89:9. They chorused to each other, "what manner of man is this, that even the wind and the sea obey him?" Mt. 8:23-27.

THE MEDIATOR HAS ARRIVED

Man was created to glory and be a friend of God when he was put in the Garden of Eden; but in complete disobedience to his maker and God, he allowed the devil to come between him and his God. Sin entered into the world, and the friendship was broken, hence man was driven out of the Garden of Eden, full of milk and honey, where everything was free of charge, where there were no worries, where there was no sickness, headache, pain, sorrow, shame nor death; there was perfect happiness.

Adam and Eve sinned, God's law was broken; life was exchanged for death; health was exchanged for sickness; plentifulness for lack and want. Man was sentenced to hard labour. This sentence, was not for a while but for "as long as man lives".

God is a righteous God, and to him righteousness should be ascribed Job 36:3. He did not spare the woman, who he sentenced to multiplication of sorrow and conception, that in sorrow shall she bring forth children; despite this, her desire shall be to her husband, and the husband shall rule over her Genesis 3:16.

And unto Adam, God said, because he hast hearkened unto the voice of his wife, and not to God's warning, and heeded his commandment, and he had eaten of the tree God had commanded "Thou shalt not eat of it; cursed is the ground for Adam's sake; in sorrow shalt he eat of it, all the days of his life. Thorns also and thistles shalt it bring forth to him, and he shalt eat the herb of the field.

In the sweat of his face shalt he eat bread till he return unto the ground; for out of it wast he taken. I know that you have not heard the story of your creation before. Look at the ground, Adam, you are dust and unto the dust shall you return Gen 3:17-19.

Humanity had sinned, and come forth short of the glory of God Rom 3:23, there is not an iota of doubt that evil has taken a stronghold over humans life. God was looking as man was doing his own things, and God doing his own. The partnership was broken and there was no more friendship position with the Creator. God was really angry and "it repented him that he had made man on the earth, and it grieved him at his heart".

And the Lord said, "I will destroy man whom I have created from the face of the earth, both man and beasts, and the creeping, and the fowls of the air; for it repents me that I have made them Gen 6:6-7.

Through his mercy, he drove them out of the garden, had he not done so, man's aspirations which leads to a new horizon would have driven them to the fruit of life, thus living forever in sin, the fruits of which is perpetual sickness and woes.

God showed them mercy by driving them out of the Garden of Eden. Since sin had entered into Adam and Eve's souls, it became inborn in their children. No one needs to call a baby to sit him down and let him know the topic of the lesson for the day "How to tell lies". A child knows "how" even before the lecture. It begins from breaking a plate, and denying it. It's not the baby talking, but the devil whose fruit is lies, for he is the father of lies working in the little child's soul and speaking through him.

I overheard a man say to his brother 'how long have you seen me telling lies". My response was "You are lying as you are speaking, because it is a lie to say you don't lie". Christ, who is above all said to the Jews "you are of your father , the devil, and the lusts of your father you will do. He was a murderer from the beginning, and abode not in truth, because there is no truth in him. When he speaks a lie, he speaks of his own; for he is a liar and the father of it John 8:44. Every liar succumbs to the devil.

Look at the man rebuking his brother, he is adding lies upon lies, therefore hell hath enlarged itself and opened her mouth without measure; and people's glory, the multitude of them all rejoicing in sins and iniquities shall enter into hell.

Note that after their fall, it is not written that Adam and Eve taught Cain to be a murderer. The devil released the spirit of jealousy to his heart, and caused him to murder his brother Abel. It was the devil that made him to be too clever by half about it, and brought the spirit of deception to conceal what happened. Asked by God "where is Abel thy brother?" he responded, "Am I my brother's keeper?" He obviously did not know that God is omniscient who knows everything. The Bible says, "for the eyes of the Lord run to and fro throughout the whole earth, to show himself strong on behalf of them whose heart is perfect toward him. Herein, thou (Cain) hast done foolishly, therefore from henceforth, thou shall have wars, (fears) 2 Chro. 16:9. God told Cain "I know what you don't know, that the voice of thy brother's blood crieth unto me from the ground, ye murderer" Gen 4: 8-10.

Man's aspirations have always turned into the new horizons. When they conquer the sea, they turned to the land, when they conquered the land they turned to the sky. When they conquer the sky, they will turn into the conquest of themselves. Man did not change outside the garden. It was from one sine to another, from iniquity to iniquity, and from transgression to transgression, so much so that "it repented God that he had made man on the earth, and it grieved him at his heart.

And the Lord said, "I will destroy man whom I have created from the face of the earth; both man and beast, and the creeping thing, and the fowls of the air; for it repenteth me that I have made them Gen. 6:6-7.

Just like two men saw fighting, throwing punches at each other, the weaker one was bruised severely, yet the stronger one did not stop throwing his punches. There came a kind man who went between them to separate them, yet the fight still continued with many blows landing on the man between them. The mediator, at the end, received more blows than the original two fighters. In most fights like this, the mediator usually gets the most beating. This man did not fight back, take sides or do anything, but try to bring peace.

It is written "O give thanks unto the Lord, for he is good, for his mercy endureth for ever" Ps 136:1. He who called a meeting in heaven with his Son and the Holy Ghost, God opening the meeting asked "What shall we do to take these our creation out of their predicaments and woe?" I can see them toiling, suffering, and labouring without profits. I see them in a state of limbo. They need redemption!

The Holy Ghost said, I know whose work this redemption should be, for he was rejoicing in the habitable part of his earth; his delight were with the sons of men Pro 8:31.

Jesus Christ spoke, and said "They are the works of our hands" Ps 143:5. "I will go and redeem these people, and just as Moses made a fiery serpent and set it upon a pole; and it came to pass that everyone that is bitten, when he looketh upon it was saved, and any man when bitten by the serpent when he beheld the serpent of brass lived, so also anyone that looked unto Jesus Christ, the Lord shall be saved". He said "Look unto me, and be ye saved, all the ends of the earth, for I am God, and there is none else" Isa 45:22.

I have sworn by myself, the word is gone out of my mouth in righteousness; and shall not return". That, unto me, every knee shall bow, every tongue shall swear Phil 2:10.

Just like the man described earlier; the Son of God came as a Mediator between his father and man. He chose to shed his blood and die for the sins of man. God hath said "Without the shedding of blood, there is no remission of sin" Heb. 9:22.

Sins abound, iniquities are free for all, just as the Bible says "Can the E-thi-opian change his skin, or the leopard his spots?" Then, may ye also do good that are accustomed to evil? Jer. 13:23. God's word is true forever. You and I can truthfully say that no man on his own can do good. Man has sinned and fallen short of the glory of God, and the wages of sin is death. However, the gift of God decided to come and redeem his people and give eternal life. Rom. 6:23.

Jesus is the one who lay down his life that he might take it again. No man taketh it from him, but he laid it down of himself. He had power to take it again. That was the commandment he received of his father John 10:17-18. May I ask for a volunteer who is ready to surrender himself today for torture, floggings and death on the stake for the offence of others? He was without sin Heb 4:15, yet he died as a substitute for sinners. He hath borne our griefs and carried our sorrows; yet, we did esteem him stricken, smitten of God, and afflicted, but he was wounded for our transgressions. He was bruised for our iniquities, the chastisement of our peace was upon him, and with his stripes we are healed Isa 53:4-5.

Apostle Peter wrote to say "Who his own self bare our sins in his own body on the tree, that we being dead to sins (absorbed, soaked, unwashable with soap, water, nor the blood of bulls, goats or calves), should live unto righteousness, by whose stripes (punishment, torture, degradation) we were healed 1 Peter 2:24, cleansed of all sins.

Reconciliation between God and man was effected, those who will look unto him will become children of God through the work of the atonement on the Calvary Cross. They will move into the spiritual realm of God; and as many as received him, to them gave he power to become the sons of God, even to them that believed in his name. Those who believe will enjoy the fruits of the Spirit which is love (agape) to God and man, joy, peace with all around and outsiders, without which no one shall see the Lord Heb 12:14, long-suffering, i.e. not easily provoked to wrath. He was an embodiment of goodness, meekness, temperance, and lowly in character.

He had reconciled us to his Father, wherefore, God also in return for his obedience, hath highly exalted him, and given him a name which is above every name that any one can mention, i.e. Moses, Elijah, Elisha, Abraham, Isaac,

Jacob, David Mohammed, Confucius, all Presidents, Prime Ministers and Kings. He is the King of Kings and Lord of Lords. 1 Tim 6:15, I testify that Jesus Christ is surely above them all.

That, at the name of Jesus, every knee, including the knee of Satan and its demons should bow, also of things in heaven (Prince of the air), and things on earth (witches, wizards, familiar spirits); for the earth is the Lord's and the fullness thereof, and they that dwell in it Psalm 24:1, and Rom. 14:11.

And every tongue, i.e. anyone with a tongue should confess that Jesus Christ is Lord. If anyone says that he believes Jesus, and cannot confess him as his Lord, such a person is of course anti-christ. Wherefore, I give you to understand that no man speaking by the Spirit of God calleth Jesus accursed; and that no man can say that Jesus is the Lord, but by the Holy Ghost 1 Cor 12:3.

The confession is done to the glory of the Father who gave us his only begotten son that whosoever believes in him as Lord and Saviour should not perish but have everlasting life, the life that was lost in the Garden of Eden John 3:16.

I pray that the Lord may bless you as you read on. Truly, Christ Jesus the Mediator has arrived.

MESSIAH IS BORN

"For unto us a child is born, unto us a son is given, the government shall be upon his shoulders, and his name shall be called Wonderful, Counsellor, the Mighty God, the Everlasting Father, Prince of Peace" Isa 9:6, "whose kingdom shall have no end."

He was born to Mary, a VIRGIN, espoused to Joseph of the house of David. His birth was different from yours and mine in that it was foretold by an angel who said to Mary that she would have a Virgin birth because she was highly favoured, that the Lord was with her, that she was blessed among women, that she would bring forth a son whose name shall be called Jesus Luke 1:27-31.

Though Mary was puzzled, she gladly accepted as she said "Behold, the handmaid of the Lord; be it unto me according to thy word. Luke 1:38.

It was again written by Isaiah the prophet that the "Lord himself shall give a sign; a virgin shall conceive and bear a son, and shall call his name Im-man-uel, which is translated GOD WITH US, who shalt know to refuse the evil and choose the good. Isaiah 7:14-15. He shall be great, and shall be called the SON OF THE HIGHEST; and the Lord God shall give unto him the throne of David, and he shall reign over the house of Jacob forever, and of his kingdom and dominion, and the greatness of the kingdom under the whole heaven, and everlasting kingdom, and all dominions shall serve and obey him Daniel 7:27. The Bible goes further to say that, "at His name, every knee shall bow" Isa. 45:23.

As soon as he was born, the wise men from the East saw his star and followed it to Jerusalem, seeking for He who was born King of the Jews. As King Herod heard of this, the spirit of jealousy and concern came upon him. He was jealous that there would be two kings in Jerusalem, not knowing that Christ's kingship was not yet due.

Concerned for his heir apparent, he had the natural view, and ordered all children under the age of two to be slaughtered; but he failed to catch his target as Jesus Christ had been taken to Egypt. The devil thus failed in his mission "no weapon that is formed against him shall prosper", and every tongue that rose up against him in judgement, he condemned for it was his heritage as the Son of God. Isa 54:17, and the Lord of Lords which he was, even before birth Luke 1:43, made him above any child that ever was born, and that would be born until he comes the second time to judge and to reign.

These three wise men went with very significant gifts, all meaningful to Christ's life and death.

Gold is the sign of Christ's kingship as the blessed and only Potentate, the King of Kings and Lord of Lords 1 Tim 6:15.

Frankincense, is the sign of his authority Mt. 7:29. He called his twelve disciples together and gave them power and authority over all devils, and to cure diseases. Luke 9:1.

Myrrh is the sign of torture and death. "He was wounded for our transgressions, he was bruised for our iniquities, the chastisement of our peace was upon him, and with his stripes we are healed Isa. 53:5, 1 Pt. 2:24.

He himself summed everything up when he said "The thief cometh not but to steal, to kill and to destroy; I am come that they might have life and that they might have it more abundantly" John 10:10, the son of God was manifested to destroy the works of the devil 1 John 3:8.

HIS CHILDHOOD

Just as his birth was unique, full of supernatural events, so also was his childhood. He was playing like any ordinary child full of life and beans, but he was never rough or rude.

He was an embodiment of goodness, but because his parents hadn't previously raised children, it was their aim that all their children would be gentle, meek, and lowly. Jesus brothers, however, were unlike him.

Christ was ever so mindful of his father's affairs. He walked strong in the spirit and was filled with wisdom and the Grace of God was with him.

I would say that he was going about in his youth making everyone that met him happy, and it was not uncommon for the parents of his friends to ask them "why can't you be like Jesus"? Jesus was a joy to his parents and all that knew him. He was indeed a true blessing to his parents and family .

A CHILD IN THE TEMPLE

It was customary of Jesus' parents to go to Jerusalem every year at the feast of the Passover.

When he was 12, an age when most children would do anything other than go to Jerusalem with their parents, Jesus was happy to go and let the people who could discern know that Christ had arrived. Jesus knew that whom he was, and he also knew that he had to go about his Father's business.

The Passover was over, the parents returned to Nazareth not knowing that the Son of God was not following them. On realising Jesus was missing, the questions "where is he?" and "what is he doing" were asked. The answer was that HE WAS IN HIS FATHER'S HOUSE.

Joseph and Mary, after a day's journey, turned back, looked everywhere and could not find him. They did not think he could be in the temple as a 12-year-old, but that was where he was, not watching what the doctors were doing but actively taking part. He sat down comfortably, asking them many searching questions which most could not answer correctly, and through questions, he was also teaching the doctors who should normally have been teaching him. The Bible says that "all that heard him were astonished at his answers, i.e. a 12 year old became their Rabbi (teacher) Luke 3:47.

Jesus was answering them beyond what they previously knew. His questions to them were so searching that he had to give clues to the answers, and they did not know that God was with them.

His parents were as astonished as the doctors, for as learned as they were, Jesus outwitted them all. Jesus' mother asked "son, why hast thou thus dealt with us? Behold, thy father and I have sought thee sorrowing". And he said unto them "sorrow not, how is it that ye sought me? Wist ye not that I must be about my father's business?" Lk. 2:46-49.

They understood not the saying which he spake unto them; that he was with the doctors for three days checking what was going on in his father's house, whether the doctors were those who knew what they were preaching, following it up with deeds, and not only with lips and mouth Mt 15:8. Mum, listen, I stayed there with them so that they may learn of me as the WISDOM OF GOD. 1 Cor. 1:24.

As said earlier, he was a source of help to everyone, the parents loved him and they often referred to him for his brothers to emulate. This made them jealous, and they tried to make Jesus angry; but instead what came out of him was, "I am going to forgive you seven times seventy times" Mt. 18:22. Today, many Christians could not do this, but for a happy living it must be done, and in addition we must turn the other cheek Mt. 5:39.

JESUS THE CARPENTER

Jesus grew up helping Joseph in his carpentry trade, and while he joined Joseph their trade boomed. Jesus became a well renowned carpenter in town, every chair, table, wardrobe that they made was of the highest quality, and always the best in town; because the Lord's work is like a tree planted by the rivers of water, that bringeth forth his fruit in his season; his leaf also shall not wither; and whatsoever he did simply prospered Psalm 1:3. So also was Jesus the carpenter.

Everyone knew that Jesus was the main contributor to Joseph's fame, and his success because before Jesus came in his work was as all other carpenters. However, Jesus introduced the hands of God into the business, and everyone noted the change. Their furniture became DESIGNER FURNITURE that everyone was seeking to buy. Any furniture not made by Jesus was really inferior. However, Joseph's furniture was affordable, neither did he or Jesus extort money from people.

The economic theory of "the greater the demand, the higher the price" never operated in Jesus trade for he is the Lord that shows compassion; one above finances.

Joseph became prosperous and renowned for. He was at the same time with God in his house, and Jesus made him prosper. 2 Chro. 26:5

Jesus was known as the Carpenter's son, he was always at the workshop helping as much as he could. People recognised Jesus so much that when he started his ministry they were surprised, saying "is not the carpenter's son, is not his mother called Mary, and his brothers James, Joseph, Simon and Judas?". They knew him and all the members in his house, and they were offended with him Mt. 13:55,57.

Jesus response to them was "I have outgrown that, I am now doing what I am sent to do in the world". The work of salvation had begun. The Bible says "A prophet is not without honour, but in his own country, and among his own kin, and in his own house Mk. 6:3-4.

Many bridegrooms who had been thinking about a piece of furniture made by Jesus as a wedding present were furious, thinking it robbery to be derived of such an opportunity to own DESIGNER FURNITURE. To them, the works of salvation was not prime, their hearts were shouting "Make us our furniture". They were inhibitive to Christ's message. They said between themselves "I know him, he made my mum's wardrobe last year", "he made my brother's chairs". They said "he is an excellent carpenter, but we don't want to hear this new doctrine he is talking about". They thus missed the GIFT OF GOD, and he therefore did not many mighty works there because of their unbelief. Mt. 13:58.

I remember when an old classmate of mine whom I had not seen for years came to one of our deliverance service at the invitation of his friend. When I came out to preach, I noticed him amongst the congregation raising his shoulders in disbelief that I, a former Muslim, was the Pastor. I got the impression that were he opportuned, he would have come out to ask "when did you become a Christian". However, the Word of God came to me "If anyone is in Christ he is a new creature. Old things are passed away, behold all things become new" 2 Cor 5:17. It seemed he got the message that I read his mind "today I am going to hear what he would say"

The message was a simple but powerful one that day, titled "Wounded for me". Obviously, all those who believed that Christ was wounded for them were all touched.

The Lord will always do what he says. In that service, a man whose belly was swollen, which was later diagnosed as a liver problem, was healed. My old classmate praised God with me, and whenever he came to town he always called at my house.

Christ will never deceive anyone, for He is the Truth. He will always show the way for he is the Way. He shows how to live a true life, for He is the Life John 14:6. His life was summed up as a High Priest who could be touched with the feeling of our infirmities; in all points, tempted like we are - YET WITHOUT SIN. Heb. 4:15.

THE MIRACLE OF JESUS

There will be a great travesty of justice if anyone talks about Jesus being above all, without rigorously mentioning his phenomenal miracles, which were performed for everyone around to see. He showed that they were not magic, he is not a trickster or a magician; he is the Son of God who asks a searching question saying "He that planted the ear shall he not hear, he that formed the eye, shall he not see?" Psalm 94:9.

Whenever he touched anyone, it is the hand of God, and miracles followed. Whenever he spoke, it was the Word of God which must accomplish that to which it was directed. No wonder he went about doing good, delivering people from their afflictions with the hand of God upon them. Neh. 2:8.

Everywhere he went, he was doing good. The mighty healer, he healed the leper with his spoken word, removing the doubt of the leper as to whether Christ would heal him or not. "I WILL cleanse you, that is why I came here; therefore be thou clean". Immediately, the leprosy was cleansed Mt. 8:2-3. Nothing is too difficult for him.

When the blind saw him, their eyes were opened. With him, nothing was difficult. When the mighty healer was passing by, he saw a man who was born blind. His disciples asked him saying "Master, who did sin, this man or his parents, that he was born blind"? Jesus answered "Neither has this man sinned, nor his parents; but that the work of God should be made manifest in him". He said "You have been following me about, seeing the work of God manifested; this is another one for your testimony. I must do the work of him (my father) that send me, while it is day; the night cometh, when no man can work. As long as I am in the world, I am the light of the world John 9:1-15, the Light which the darkness cannot comprehend".

He spat on the ground, and with the hand of God, which are the hands of power, he made clay of the spittle, and anointed the eyes of the blind man with the clay.

Jesus said unto him "Go wash in the pool of Siloam". The blind went his way and came back seeing. Just as it is human to pick a choice between the truth and lies, many said it was the blind man, others thought it was impossible for a person born blind to recover their sight. This was beyond their imagination. They seemed to prefer this man to remain blind than to see. They never thanked God for him, because they perceived that it was Jesus who performed such a miracle.

The conversation that followed could not have arisen if the miracle was performed by one of the Pharisees, the challenge to Jesus which was baseless was "Sabbath", of which Christ is the Lord, i.e. they asked Christ "Why did you heal on Sabbath day, why not next Friday"? The funny thing was that those hypocrites had Monday to Friday to themselves, but could not heal a donkey, never mind healing the blind.

There was much rift on this, the blind man's parents were called to confirm whether the man who they had been giving alms was born blind. The parents confirmed he was born blind, and that he was their son. "We don't want to get involved in this Sabbath business, don't bother us, we don't know by whose hand this joy came to us, but we are very happy".

Still in awe, they went back again to the man who had just received his sight "tell us by your mouth that he who has done this marvel is a sinner". "Tell us so that we shall be satisfied and give glory to Sabbath".

The blind man who now could see said "That is your business, nothing concerns me with this Sabbath, it is the day of my joy as it is today and I will give praise to God". He said "I don't know whether he is a sinner or not, all I know is I was blind and I can now see; I believe you know that a sinner could not wrought this great miracle.

When things unexpected do happen, it is natural to wonder, how? where? when and who? They pestered the man with questions, but he gave them the same answer "I perceive you would like to learn his method for when you meet a blind man, hence you continually ask these irrelevant questions. One thing I do know is that, unless Jesus gives the power, you won't be able to do anything like this". "Would you also be his disciples", he asked.

The Pharisees reviled him and said, we can't blame you much that "thou art his disciple, but we are Moses' disciples", who is inferior to Jesus Heb. 3:3. For this man you rejected was counted worthy of more glory than Moses, inasmuch as he who hath built the house has more honour than the house, you chose wrongly.

We know that God spake unto Moses, as for this fellow, we know not from whence he is. Christ had once answered this irritating question; "Though I bear record of myself, yet my record is true; for I know whence I came, and whither I go; but ye cannot tell whence I come and whither I go". John 8:14.

The man could not be questioned. Why all this rigmarole? Herein is a marvellous thing that ye know not from whence he is, for ye lack the knowledge of discernment. I tell you once more that he hath opened mine eyes.

You do know, as I do, that God heareth not sinners. For his eyes are purer than to behold evil, and cannot look unto iniquity Habakkuk 1:13; but if any man be a worshipper of God and doeth his will, him he heareth.

I know that you know that since the world began, was it not heard that any man opened the eyes of one that was born blind. Let us speak the truth to ourselves. If this man were not of God, he could do nothing.

Their conclusion was "you too are a sinner, don't teach us" John 9:1-34. Instead of praising God, they then cast him out.

THE DEAF AND DUMB CURED

And the Lord said unto him "Who hath made man's mouth? Or who maketh the dumb or deaf, or the seeing or the blind? Have not I, the Lord? Exo. 4:11.

Christ continued his going about and doing good. Departing from the coasts of Tyre and Sidon, he came unto the sea of Galilee, through the midst of the coasts of Decapolis.

And they brought unto him one that was deaf, and had an impediment in his speech; and they beseeched him to put his hand upon him, recognising that his hand is the hand of God.

The Lord above all impediments took the man aside from the multitude, and put his healing hands into the man's ears, and he spit and touched his tongue. Looking into heaven he sighed and said to him "E-ph-pha-tha", i.e. "be opened".

Straightaway, his ears were opened and the strings of his tongue was loosed, and he spoke plain language. "Thank you Lord, I can hear what everybody is saying" he said. He went on his way saying to people "I am no more deaf, I have met Jesus, I am now a new man". He invited people to listen to him, testing his newfound freedom from the power of darkness. He discussed with people what God had done for him Mk. 7:31-37.

THAT WAS THE MARRIAGE THAT WAS

The Bible says that "As it is written, Behold, I lay in Si-on a stumbling stone and rock of offence; and whosoever believeth on him shall not be ashamed. Rom. 9:33.

Many people know that marriage is honourable, but the first day of marriage can be dishonourable and shameful if not properly planned. More so, when the guests could not be satisfied with food and drink.

A young man was getting married, he invited many guests, but many more turned up. How blessed was he that Jesus was present, even though nobody else recognised who he was, save his mother.

The people were wining and dining happily until the wine barrels dried up. The bridegroom's friends were running helter skelter, but there was nowhere to buy any more wine. The seed of shame was firmly planted and people began to compare the wedding to previous weddings they had attended where there was more than enough drink for everybody.

Mary, mother of Jesus, was also concerned. Knowing the type of son that she had, she called him aside "They have no wine, have compassion on them". She said "I know that you can do it, please remove the reproach from this couple lest people laugh at them and ask them where are you their God". Ps. 119:22.

Jesus then turned unto his mother saying "Woman! What have I to do with thee? Mine hour is not yet come". Interestingly, the mother did not take "no" for an answer but said to the servants "Whatsoever he says unto you, do it". The servants were probably questioning in their minds "Who is he that we should obey him, what can he ask us to do now?". They probably weren't concerned since the shame wasn't theirs, but of the newly married couple. Nevertheless, they obeyed Christ's instructions to "fill the waterpots with water", and they filled them up to the brim.

And he said unto them "Draw out now, and bear unto the governor of the feast". They did obey, and they bare it.

You would like to know what happened; the ruler of the feast tasted the water that was made wine, and not whence it was. He called the bridegroom and said unto him "every man at the beginning doth set forth good wine; and when men have well drunk, then that which is worse; but thou hast kept the good wine until now". Hallelujah. All the prophets before him were equally not as good, for where the Spirit of the Lord is, there is liberty. Christ who is above all problems was then around and reproach, contempt, and shame must flee, for he was able and is still more than able to deliver us from anything contrary to our welfare if we trust in him John 2:1-11.

CAN YOU FACE THE DESTROYER ALONE?

The Word of God, which is alive, says unto Ze-rub-ba-bel "Not by might, nor by physical power, but by my spirit saith the Lord of Hosts" Zech. 4:6.

The Lord was in the synagogue with all the big guns. He taught them even though many were as old as Methuselah. He taught them just as he did at the age of twelve, and they were astonished at his doctrine, which none of them could match. He taught them as one that had authority, and not as the scribes with D.D. etc in theology.

There had been in the synagogue a man with an unclean spirit for a long time, who none of the scribes with all their knowledge and outward godly outlook could heal. He cried out with a loud voice saying "let us alone, what have we done with thee, thou Jesus of Nazareth? Art thou come to destroy us? I know thee who thou are, the HOLY ONE OF GOD".

They said that they cannot be equally yoked together, what fellowship have they with Jesus? You are righteous, and they are unrighteous. They asked him "what communion hath you, Jesus as light, with darkness". "What concord hath you, Christ, with Belial, the Master of the unclean spirits"? What part hath he that believeth with an infidel? 2 Cor 6:14-15.

And Christ rebuked him, saying "Shut up, hold thy peace, and come out of him" Mk. 1:25. And when the unclean spirit had torn him, and cried with a loud voice, he came out of him, and they were all amazed in so much that they questioned among themselves, saying "what thing is this, what new doctrine is this"? For with authority commandeth he even the unclean spirits, and they do obey him.

And immediately his fame spread abroad throughout all the region, round about Galilee. People said "Take all your problems to Jesus; cast all of them to him for he cares for you" 1 Peter 5:7.

The Scribes were envious as the market of lies was closing up fast. The stock was losing its value. There were not so many customers as in the past. People were rushing to Jesus who said "My sheep hear my voice, and I know them, and they follow me, and I give unto them eternal life; and they shall never perish, neither shall any man pluck them out of my hand. The devil tried to pluck this man, but I have come to release him from this bondage you now all see" John 10:27-28, Mk. 1:22-28.

THE DEVILS ALSO BELIEVED AND TREMBLED

It is written "Thou believest that there is one God; thou doest well; the devils who ought not to, also believed, and recognising the power and wrath of God, they trembled and obeyed the commandments when they are cast out to wherever we, as children of God command them to go in Jesus name" James 2:19.

There was a day when Jesus and all his followers went over unto the other side of the sea, into the country of the Gadarenes.

He was not met by crowds of well wishers, but by a man who had made the tombs his home.

I believe that no one would willingly make such a frightful place his home, particularly at night! However, this was his own home, Jesus Christ said that "The thief (the devil) cometh not, but for to kill, steal and destroy". The devil steals the money or property of its victim, torments him at will, and then destroys the victim together with himself in hell.

This man of Gandarene had gone beyond depression and oppression, and he was in the final stage of possession by the devil, who honoured him with legions of his demons. No man could bind him, no not with chains, all which are handiworks of men. It was obvious that no one could fight the spiritual with the natural, the physicians, herbalists, and all the doctors in Gadarene have tried, but failed, therefore the man was left to his own so called fate. To them, he was beyond healing.

He was always in the mountains, cutting himself with stones all night and day. He was nicknamed "The terror of the mountain". He had the control of that region, such that people were afraid to bury people in that cemetery anymore.

But when he saw Jesus afar off, he ran and worshipped him, and cried with a loud voice, trembling and saying "What have I to do with thee, Jesus, thou SON OF THE MOST HIGH GOD"? " I adjure thee by God that thou torment me not".

He commanded the unclean spirits to "Come out of that man", and asked him "What is they name". And he answered, saying his name is Legion "for there are more than two thousand demons". And he besought him, Jesus, much not to send them away. He knew that they were out but not cast away. When you rebuke and bind, know that the demons are out and still around. They need to be cast out to a specific place, and they must obey at the name of Jesus (Amen).

Then, there were unto the mountains, a great herd of swine about three thousand of them feeding, and all the demons besought him to send them into the swine, that they may enter into them; clever by half, they did not want to go into the sea.

And immediately, "Jesus gave them leave and the unclean spirits went out, and entered into the swine, and the herd ran violently down a steep place into the sea and were choked in the sea".

They that fed the swine fled to the city, and informed the people of the wonderful event. They said "This man Jesus had no weapon to frighten the swine with, he simply said GO, and they departed from the man". They were all angry that they had lost all their swine, but a man's soul cannot be compared to a billion swine or can it?

The relatives of the mad man called others that they had a report that their relative nicknamed 'terror at the tomb' is cured'. They marvelled that the top physician had failed to cure him, yet someone else had cured him. There was a stampede to go to the tomb to meet the healer.

They came to Jesus and saw him that was possessed with the devil, and had the legion sitting, for with God, nothing shall be impossible Luke 1:37. He was clothed, rags taken off, and he had linen and woollen attires on him. He was answering questions correctly, recognising who they were. It wasn't a dream, but true!

They were needlessly afraid as they heard the testimony of the deliverance from the power of the devil. The transfer to the swine; the swine and devil's demise in the sea.

Instead of praising God and rejoicing with the mad man then healed, they said that the power was too much to remain in their country. They reckoned that if God was around, the devil would have none to torment; the physicians, herbalists, and traditional medical men would be out of business. They pleaded with Jesus to leave their coast.

The mad man who was now healed recognised that as long as Jesus is around there would be no demon to torment him anymore; he therefore offered to remain with Jesus. You have been delivered from the power of darkness, and translated into the kingdom of his dear son Col. 1:13. The question is, "do you want to remain with Jesus who is above all principalities and powers"? He commanded the man to go home to his friends and tell them how great things the Lord had done for him, and hath compassion on him. Mark 5:1-19.

THE WONDERFUL SUPPLIER

We now recognise that wherever Jesus went, there would be a multitude of people. He went to the sea of Galilee, and went up into a mountain and sat down there. At the place were great multitudes.

Amongst them were the lame, blind, deaf, dumb and maimed with many diverse diseases. They simply cast them at Jesus feet. "Here you are, help us, for who else can we run to?" they asked.

The compassionate Jesus healed them all. None was left untouched, and people wondered when they saw the dumb speak, the maimed made whole, the lame walk, and the blind see; and they glorified the God of Israel.

The programme had been on for three days, remember that there were no hawkers on the mountain tops, and what was going on was beyond thinking of any other things. When people saw a lame person leap up there were shouts of joy, people went without food and fasted without even knowing it.

After three days, people realised that they had to go home to eat. They had not hungered because "In the presence of God, there is fullness of joy", but they now needed food to eat which Jesus was about to supply.

Because of the distance to the market in town, and because of the financial constraints, Jesus disciples said unto him "we know that you can do marvels but what you are talking about seems gigantic". Where can we find so much bread in the wilderness, as to fill so great a multitude?

Jesus said unto them, "How many loaves have ye"? They answered, "seven, and a few little fishes".

Jesus commanded the multitude to sit down on the ground, and he took the seven loaves and the fish, and gave thanks, and broke them and gave to his disciples, and they to the multitude.

And they did all eat, and were filled; and they took up of the broken meat that was left, seven baskets full. And the people that ate were four thousand men. I will add two thousand women, and four thousand children, say about ten thousand people in all.

Christ shall meet your needs which are causing you concern today. He is the wonderful supplier that brought the voice of joy, and the voice of gladness, the voice of the bridegroom, and the voice of the bride, the voice of them that shall say "Praise the Lord of hosts"; for the Lord is good; for his mercy endureth forever Jere. 33:11(a).

Obviously, this seems impossible for man, but to God it is very easy. We are in the additional method of prosperity, but Christ is not in this method. He is in the multiplication method of doing things.

When we add $5 + 5$ we get 10.

God, however multiplies 5×5 to get 25. Same numbers, different results. The greater the numbers used, the higher the difference in your result to God's result i.e. $100 + 100 = 200$, God's $100 \times 100 = 10,000$.

God is higher than any situation, and with one touch your present problems, however great they might seem, will vanish in Jesus name.

Always remember that Christ fed about eleven thousand people with seven loaves and a few fishes, and there were seven full baskets left over. Mt. 15: 29-38.

After these things, Jesus went over the sea of Galilee which is the sea of Tiberias. Great multitudes followed him, because they saw his miracles which he did on them that were diseased. When they needed food, in this instance there were only five barley loaves and two small fishes. Again, Jesus wrought the same miracle.

He asked his disciples to make the people sit down, and he shared the food amongst them.

This time, there were twelve baskets left over. Surely, the Lord Jesus is above poverty and hunger.

WHY JESUS CAME

For all have sinned and come short of the glory of God Rom. 3:23.

And you and I are in no wise cleaner than Adam and Eve in the garden of Eden. It has been proved by our fruits, both Jews and Gentiles, that we are all under sin.

As it is written "There is none righteous, no not one". "There is none that understandeth, there is none that seeketh after God". It is still true today.

"Everyone had gone out of the way, they are together become unprofitable; there is none that doeth good, no, not one" Rom. 3:9-12.

The punishment for the sin of man is death, complete annihilation from the presence of God Almighty, to the hand of the devil as the bondmaster with all his atrocities; sickness, poverty, lacks and wants. Man is spiritually dead, and man became completely earthly, thereby dancing to only one music i.e. the music of the devil with sexual perversion, material lust leading to armed robbery, pilfering, lies and deceits.

The Bible summed it all up for all to see, commanding us to adjust to God's way, who is Jesus Christ.

"Know ye not that the unrighteous do not inherit the Kingdom of God?" Be not deceived, neither fornicators, nor idolaters, nor adulterers, nor effeminate, i.e. homosexuals, bisexuals, nor abusers of themselves with mankind".

Nor thieves, nor covetous, nor drunkards, nor revilers, nor extortioners shall inherit the Kingdom of God 1 Cor. 6: 9-10.

Man is full of the works of the flesh, which manifests from time to time.

Adultery, fornication, uncleanness, lasciviousness, witchcraft, hatred, variance, emulations, strife, seductions, heresies, envyings, murders, revellings; of such they which do such things shall not inherit the Kingdom of God. Their inheritance is of Satan, which is hell-fire.

Don't let us deceive ourselves, for such were some of you; but ye are washed, but ye are sanctified, but ye are justified in the name of the Lord Jesus, and by the Spirit of our God 1 Cor. 6:11.

When we look at the above listed sins, we could ask ourselves "who then shall be saved from the wrath of God"?

I say, be happy that Jesus Christ who is above death in that he swallowed up death in victory, through resurrection, and was without sin, had taken our place. While we were yet sinners, Christ died for us. He died for us that we should live together with him 1 Thes. 5:10.

We must know it that He is the Gift of God who gives the Eternal Life, for He Himself is Life John 14:6.

He came to this sinful world to save sinners, because whoever commits sin (who doesn't?) is of the devil; for the devil sinned from the beginning, and was cast down from heaven by the blood of the Lamb; and came to make man sin and became his property; for the purpose of a mighty redemption, the Son of God was manifested, that he might destroy the works of the devil 1 John 3:8.

He therefore redeems our lives from destruction; and crowned us with loving kindness and tender mercies. He satisfies our mouths with good things; so that our youths be renewed like the eagles Ps. 103: 4-5.

He came and delivered us from the power of darkness, and hath translated us into his Kingdom; and in him we have redemption through the blood he shed on the Calvary Cross, flowing for the forgiveness of sins Col. 1:13-14.

He came to restore us to God, who commands his love towards us in that, while we were yet sinners, Christ who was sinless died for us; we are justified by his blood. We shall be saved from the wrath of God through him, and him alone.

As enemies of God, we were reconciled to Him by the death of his Son, and much more, being reconciled, we shall be saved by his life. Rom. 5:8-10.

And you know what? You who were afar off are made nigh by the blood of Jesus Christ who is our peace who broke down the middle wall of partition between us and God. He, on our behalf, abolished in his flesh the enmity; abrogated the law of commandments contained in the ordinances of Moses to combine the two. The two covenants, i.e. the old and new were made by the blood of Jesus to become one, and through this we have peace with God. Eph. 2: 13-15.

To enjoy all the good things by him, you must cast all your cares upon him, for he cares for you. Your own part is to be sober and vigilant for the devices of the devil, for which you must not be ignorant. For the devil, as a roaring lion which the Lion of Judah had defeated, walks about seeking whom he may devour. Remember, also that the devil is a defeated foe 1 Peter 5:8-10.

Christ is the Door of hope. He is the Door of faith. The Door to reach the Father, the Door of Mansions prepared for us in his Father's house for us that do his will, all that know that Jesus Christ is the Son of the Ever living God. He is above everything, surely He that cometh from above is above all.

THIS IS MY BELOVED SON

And He said unto them, "Verily, I say unto you that there be some of you that stand here, which shall not taste death till they have seen the kingdom of God come with power. How could that happen? Only by taking some of them to see him in glory.

"For the Son of Man shall come in the glory of his Father with his angels, and then shall reward every man according to his works".
Verily, I say unto you, there be some standing here which shall not taste of death till they see the Son of Man coming in his Kingdom.

He took Peter, James, and John and led them up onto a high mountain, and he was transfigured before them; revealing how He shall be in glory with them, his raiment shining, and as white as snow, and his face did shine as the sun.

There appeared unto them E-Li-as with Moses, talking with Jesus about his death, which he should meet at Jerusalem Luke 9:31, his time almost accomplished.

Peter answered, and said to Jesus "Master, it is good for us to be here, we have seen the Kingdom of God come with power, we have also seen you in your glory, therefore let us make three tabernacles; one for thee, one for Moses, and one for Elias who we see with thee".

While he yet spoke, there came a cloud and overshadowed them; and they feared as they entered into the cloud Lk 9:34.

And there came a voice out of the cloud saying "This is my beloved son, hear him" Mk. 9:7, for he is greater and above Elias and Moses you saw with him, he is above all prophets Heb. 1:1-3.

And suddenly, when they had looked round about, they saw no man anymore, save Jesus only with themselves.

And Jesus charged them saying "Tell the vision to no man, until the Son of Man be risen again from the dead". Thus Peter, James and John saw the Kingdom of God come with power. I have the feeling that because of what they did see, Peter made a vow that he could not fulfil; i.e. that come rain or sunshine, he would be with his master and die with him, and not for him as it came to be at last. Thus Christ is confirmed to be above Moses and Elias by God the Father.

TO WHOM CAN YOU COMPARE HIM?

Christ is the Lord God Almighty Rev. 1:8 whose name and power is known among the heathens; the Christians are rightly called Believers; they must know that they are not the only believers.

God's arch enemy, the devil believeth each time he hears the mighty name of Jesus, he is shaken and frightened right down to his bones, and of course he trembles James 2:19.

Jesus has been called a Warrior, Saviour, Victor, Helper and the one whose name is above all names.

Genesis:	He is known as the seed of the woman - Gen. 3:15.
Exodus:	Lamb without blemish - Lev. 1:3.
Numbers:	Pillar of Cloud by day and Pillar of Light by night - Num. 9:16.
Deuteronomy:	Prophet unto like Moses - Deut. 18:15.
Joshua:	Captain of the host of the Lord - Josh. 5:14
Judges:	Judge and Deliverer - Jdg. 2:16
Ruth:	Kinsman and Redeemer - Ruth 2:1
Samuel:	Faithful Priest - 1 Sam. 2:35
Kings:	Lord, the King - 1 King 1:2
Chronicles:	Chief of Levites - 1 Chro. 15:16
Ezra:	Chief of Fathers of Judah. - Ezra 1:5
Nehemiah:	Faithful Priest - Neh. - 8:2
Esther:	Mor-de-cai; the Deliverer - Esth. 6:11
Job:	Wonderful Redeemer - Job 5:20
Psalms:	The Lord our Shepherd - Ps. 23:1
Proverbs:	Wisdom of God - Prov. 8
Ecclesiastes:	The Preacher - Eccle. 1:1
Solomon:	Rose of Sharon & Lily of the Valley - Sol. 2:1
Isaiah:	The Prince of Peace - Isa. 9:6
Jeremiah:	Weeping Prophet - Jer. 31:15
Ezekiel:	Son of Man - Ezek. 2:13

Daniel:	The 4th Man in the Fiery Furnace - Dan 3:5
Hosea:	Everlasting Husband - Hos. 3:1
Joel:	Holy Spirit Baptizer - Joel 2:28
Amos:	Tabernacle of David - Amos 9:11
Obadiah:	Saviour - vs. 21
Jonah:	The run away Prophet - Jon. 1:3
Micah:	The Lord Redeemer - Mic. 4:10
Nahum:	Our Avenger - Nah. 1:2
Habakkuk:	Evangelist praying for revival - Hab. 3:2
Zephaniah:	Our Lord who is mighty to save - 3:17
Haggai:	The Laid Precious Stone - Haggai 2:15
Zechariah:	Fountain Open to the House of David - Zech 13:1
Malachi:	Sun of Righteousness - Mal. 4:2

We can all see how the Old Testament prophets valued and recognised the role played by Jesus the Lord in the lives of his people in their times. The names indicated how much he cared, and I say that today, he still cares.

In the New Testament, his caring attitude continued, even to the point of death, the death on the cross. Phil. 2:8

Matthew:	Emmanuel, i.e. God with us - Matt 1:23.
Mark:	Mighty miracle worker - Mark 5:1-43.
Luke:	Son of Peace - Luke 10:6.
John:	Son of God - John 1:34.
Acts:	The Lord whose name saves - Acts 4:12.
Romans:	The Justifier - Rom 3:24.
Corinthians:	Sanctifier - 1 Cor. 1:2.
Galatians:	Redeemer from the curse of the Law - Gal. 3:13.
Ephesians:	The name above every other name - Eph. 1:21.
Philippians:	The Lord that supplies our needs - Phil. 4:19.
Colossians:	Head of the Church - Col. 1:18.
Thessalonians:	The soon coming Christ - 2 Thes. 2:2.
Timothy:	Mediator between God and men - 1 Tim. 2:5.
Titus:	God that cannot lie - Titus 1:2..
Philemon:	Friend of the Prisoner - Vs. 9.
Hebrews:	Consecrated Son of God for ever more - Heb. 7:28
James:	The Lord who raises up the sick - James 5:15.
Peter:	The soon coming Chief Shepherd - 1 Ptr. 5:4.
1 John:	Christ who first loved us - 1 Jn. 4:19.
Jude:	The Lord coming with ten thousands of his saints - Vs. 14.
Revelations:	King of Kings and Lord of Lords - Rev. 17:14.

It was not an exaggeration when Paul the Apostle wrote that "Jesus sanctifies the people with his own blood, and he is the same yesterday, today and forever" Heb. 13:8.

Be not deceived by human thoughts to doubt his Deity, for he is the Alpha and Omega, the beginning and the end, which was, and is, and which is to come, THE ALMIGHTY Rev. 1:8.

Let us yield to his calling. He is the one that lived, and was dead, crucified on the Calvary Cross, and we know for a fact that "He is alive for evermore". He has the keys of hell and death; and your judgement is in his hand. Rev. 1:18, John 5:22.

Who can be likened to him who started the obliteration of the wages of sin in the Garden of Gethsemane, and completed it by going to the cross. From there, to the grave, and the power to the grave failed to hold him. He resurrected and finally ascended to heaven, sitting on the right hand of God, shining as the sun of righteousness Mal. 4:2.

The Bible tells us that the Lord's power is incomparable, for he is greater than all the gods combined together; for in the things where their believers claim to be great, and they dealt proudly; Jesus is above them. He came to destroy all their works which by all accounts are evil 1 John 3:8.

He is the only embodiment of power, for he received all power in heaven and earth. No one else has power, he stripped the devil and his demons of whatever power they had, and spoiled principalities and powers, made a show of them openly, and triumphing over them in it. Col. 2:15. It means that when faced with anything which is the work of the devil; you plead the blood, with the name of Jesus, and the result is victory for you. Simply draw out of the Lord's power and the effect is swifter than an eagle. Witches, familiar spirits, all principalities and powers of darkness, and spiritual wickedness in high places do bow at the name of Jesus for he is above them all.

He is ready to help whoever comes to him, and such would not perish, and will be protected here on earth and given eternal life; which none of the religious leaders guaranteed to their followers.

He said that he, as the Son of God was not sent into the world to condemn it but, rather that the world might be saved through him. He who believeth on him is not condemned, but he that believeth not is condemned already because he hath not believed in the only begotten Son of God John 3:18.

John the Baptist rounded it up by saying "Jesus, that cometh from above is above all". He that is of the earth, created with soil is earthly, and could not readily understand heavenly things; he that cometh from above; the throne of God Almighty is heavenly and above all John 3:31.

You have a part to play, which is for you to believe in who his Father sent from above to be our Lord and Saviour; who hath measured the waters in the hollow of his hand, and meted out heaven with the span, and understand the dust of the earth in a measure, and weighed the mountains in scales, and the hills in abundance.

No one hath directed his Spirit or any one being his advisor or teacher, he had none to show him what to do or advise him how to judge righteously, or the way of knowledge; he needed none for he himself is above all of them.

To him, the nations are as a drop of a bucket, and are counted as the small dust of the balance; behold he taketh up the isles as a very little thing. Lebanon is not sufficient to burn, nor the beasts thereof sufficient for a burnt offering.

All nations before him are as nothing; and they are counted to him less than nothing, and vanity.

Finally, to whom then will you liken him, or what likeness will you compare unto him who is from above, and above all.

TO WHO CAN YOU COMPARE HIM?

The Lord God of Hosts asks a question which I would like you to answer now "To whom will you liken me, and make me equal, and compare me that we may be like?" Isaiah 46:5.

It came to pass, when Jesus returned from Godarene, the people welcomed him gladly, for they were waiting for him, obviously to receive of him.

A ruler of the synagogue, named Jairus, came in and fell down at Jesus' feet and begged him that he would come into his house, for he had only one twelve year old daughter. The girl lay dying, barely breathing when her father came to Jesus.

Jesus being compassionate was ready to go immediately with Jairus, but there were so many people thronging around him. However, a woman suffering from cancer of the womb for twelve years, who had been deprived of her livelihood, whose family were all in debt because of her, the devil had stolen their wealth.

The woman had tried everything, x-rays upon x-rays, diagnosis upon diagnosis. The medical students had a field day trying to diagnose her case.

This woman, on the point of desperation, decided to get to Jesus and do something that no one had done before. "What shall I do?" she said. "If I touch the helm of his garment, I am sure that I will be healed, and he won't know that I have touched him". She was very wrong for as soon as she touched Jesus, virtue went out of him, and she was immediately healed.

Jesus asked "Who touched me among the crowd"? Everyone denied it, including the woman who could have gone out jumping and praising the Lord that the battle had been won. Peter unknowingly covered up for her. "Master, see how huge the crowd is, how can you know who among these touched you", he said "It can't have been deliberate". Jesus said "No, you are wrong, Peter. I know because healing flowed out of me to someone".

The woman came out trembling and confessed everything that happened to her, Peter knew that Christ cannot lie Heb. 6:18a.

Meanwhile, Jairus was getting impatient that the woman came and delayed Jesus, this preventing his daughter's healing. It did not take long but while Jesus was talking, a servant from the ruler of the synagogue came to give a message telling Jairus' of the bereavement of his daughter. "Trouble not the master. Thy daughter is dead, we tried everything that we could".

Jairus was obviously furious with the woman with the issue of blood that she had delayed Jesus, thinking that if she hadn't his daughter would have lived. He couldn't believe his ears when Jesus said "Fear not; believe only, and she shall be made whole".

Jairus hopes rose, "I have seen a miracle performed on that woman, if you say so, my daughter would be raised". When Jesus came to the house, he suffered no man to go in, save Peter and James, and John and the parents of the maiden. All wept and bewailed her, but he said "Weep not, she is not dead but sleepeth". They all laughed him to scorn, knowing that she had been dead for quite a while. Some who didn't know Jesus were asking "Who is this man who cannot recognise the dead"? The doctor had certified her dead, her pulse had been taken, and she was officially dead.

Jesus put them all out because their faith was not strong enough, and then he took the dead daughter by the hand and said "Maid arise" (Hallelujah).

And her spirit came again, and she arose straight away; and he commanded them to give her meat. Her parents, as well as those who scorned him, were astonished Lk. 8:41-56). They praised God with Jairus, and obviously the scorners were put to open shame.

Another day came, another only child, a boy was dead when Jesus was passing through his city in Na-in. As usual, many of the disciples went with him, as well as a large crowd.

There was sorrow in the city for the only son of a widow was dead. Whilst the body was being carried to the graveyard, they met Christ the Resurrection and the Life at the gates to the city. When Jesus saw the widow, he had compassion on her and said to her "Weep not". No doubt, the mourners would have thought "doesn't he know that her only remaining hope in life had gone"

The Bible says that "If a man beget a hundred children, and live many years, so that the days of his years be many, and his soul be not filled with good, and also that he have no burial; an untimely birth is better than he" Ecc l6:3.

And Jesus came and touched the bier; and they that bare him stood still. And he said, "Young man, I the Lord above death say unto thee, Arise". And the boy that was dead sat up and began to speak, and Jesus delivered him to his mother whose sorrow turned to great joy.

There was a great fear on all, and they praised and glorified God, saying that "a great prophet is risen among us"; but Christ is greater than any prophets. At times past, God at sundry times, and in divers manners spoke to the fathers by the prophets and hath in these last days spoken unto us by his Son whom he hath appointed heir of all things, by whom also he made the worlds.

Who, being the brightness of his glory, and the express image of his person, and upholding all things by the word of his power, when he had by himself purged all our sins, sat down on the right hand of the Majesty on high Heb. 1:1-3. Thus, Christ is better and greater than any prophets.

Be it known to you that the Son of God is surely above all prophets.

HE CALLED THE DEAD OUT OF THE GRAVE

We have seen Jesus who raised up the dead in the room. We have seen him raise up the dead on the way to the burial ground. Now we will see the dead already buried, and he came on the fourth day to raise him up.

Now Lazarus, the brother of Mary and Martha was sick. The sisters send to Jesus saying, "Lord, behold, he whom thou lovest is sick". They expected him to come quickly to heal his friend. He did not do that. He was talking already of the would be outcome of the sickness, that it was that the Son of God might be glorified thereby.

Instead of rushing to heal Lazarus, he abode two days still in the same place where he was. After these two days, he asked the disciples to follow him to Judea again where the Jews sought to stone him. He gave them talk on what time to walk about, which is in the light, for he is the Light. Jesus then told them the time that Lazarus passed away; by saying "Our friend Lazarus sleepeth, but we go that I may awake him out of sleep".

The disciples did not know that Christ was saying that Lazarus was dead, but one thing is that he was glad for their sakes that he was not there to heal him. It was for them to believe that Jesus is truly the Resurrection and the Life.

The doubting Thomas's came in as usual, and when Jesus got there Lazarus had lain the grave for four days already.

When Martha saw Jesus coming she went to meet him, but Mary remained in the house.

Martha, still in the realm of time thought it was too late for Jesus to perform miracles and said "I am quite sure that he would still be alive now if you had been here four days ago; but I know now that whatever thou wilt ask now, God will give it to thee". Martha could see a healer, but not the Resurrection and the Life. Then Jesus said unto her, "Thy brother shall rise again". Martha agreed with him, thinking Jesus meant on the resurrection day.

Jesus said to her "I am the Resurrection and the Life, he that believes in me, though he were dead, yet shall he live". He said "And whosoever believes in me shall never die. Surely, verily verily I say unto you, if a man keep my saying, he shall never see death".

Martha said "Yea Lord, I believe that thou are the Christ the Son of God, which should come into the world". She then went and called Mary.

The Jews with Mary followed her to meet Jesus, and then they went to the grave to weep there. Mary also repeated Martha's word "If thou had been here, my brother would not have died". Jesus groaned in his spirit as he saw her weeping along with other Jews. He wept with them to show that he shared their grief John

11:35. Then it was time for Lazarus to be delivered from the cold hand of death and the grave.

Jesus said "Take ye away the stone". Martha reminded Jesus that the body which had lain in the grave for four days would now be stinking. Jesus reminded her that he had told her that "If thou believe, thou shall see the glory of God".

Then they took away the stone from the place where the dead was laid, and Jesus lifted up his eyes and said "Father, I thank thee that thou hast heard me. And I know that thou hears me always but; because of the people which stand by, I said it that they may believe, that thou hast sent me" John 11:42.

And when he thus had spoken, he cried with a loud voice "Lazarus, come forth. Verily, verily I say unto you, the hour is coming and now is when the dead shall hear the voice of the Son of God; and they that hear shall live".

"For as the Father hath life in himself; so hath he given to the Son to have life in himself" John 5: 25-26.

And Lazarus that was dead came forth, bound hand and foot with grave clothes, and his face was bound about with a napkin. Jesus said unto them "Loose him and let him go".

Like Naaman, the leper, Lazarus body was like that of a new born baby with his spirit restored to him. Truly Jesus Christ is the Resurrection and the Life, who is above death and the power of the grave.

THE BATTLE GROUND

I have put you on the scale and found you wanting. You are worthless in terms of the Kingdom of God. Yet you know not the worst state of your spiritual destitution Jer. 50:24.

The above was directed to the Pharisees who always pitched battle with Jesus. They didn't have anything in common with Jesus but, rather, were the "holier than thou" sect. No one was as 'holy' as them. They expected other people's obeisance because of their holiness, and everything they did was after the tradition of men "Matt. 15:3".

Their piety was to impress people, thus leaving the right things undone. Because Jesus corrected them, they took him as enemy number 1.

They liked to receive God's glory for themselves, to which Jesus objected. "I am the Lord, that is my name, and my glory will I not give to another, neither my praise to graven images" Isa. 42:8.

In Luke 18:9-14, you see the Pharisee's arrogant and egoistic prayer, how he claimed righteousness, the holier than thou attitude he took towards the publican as a 'sinner' who did not fast two times a week.

The Pharisee was so righteous that he could not see that only God is good Lk. 18:19.

The Pharisees were so pompous that they challenged everybody, including God, asking why the disciples transgressed the tradition of the elders by not washing their hands when they ate bread. Jesus answered them "Why do ye also transgress the commandment of God by your tradition. You have made the commandment of God of no effect by your tradition" Mt. 15 3:6.
"Ye hypocrites, well did Esias prophesy of you saying; these people draw nigh unto me with their lips; but their heart is far from me" Mt. 15:8. The Pharisees shouted "Hear him, what he said about us".

The Bible says that the Pharisee received nothing from God, and the publican went home justified. The publican was aware that "all have sinned and come short of the glory of God" Rom. 3:23. He knew that, if we confess our sins, he is faithful and just to forgive us our sins, and to cleanse us from all unrighteousness 1 John 1:9.

The Pharisees caught a woman in adultery. They could judge according to Moses' law to stone her to death; but to entrap their Lord and God, they asked Jesus to judge her. Jesus told them that his judgement is righteous, he knew their traps laid for him. If he had said they should stone her to death, they would have said he was not merciful, nor compassionate; and if he had said they should let her go, they would have accused him of breaking the law.

Christ, who is above all human traps turned to them to judge themselves. "He that is without sin among you, let him first cast a stone at her" John 8:7. The accusers that heard it, being convicted by their own conscience went out one by one, until Jesus was left alone with the woman. Jesus then told the woman to "Sin no more" John 8:9-11.

He told the Pharisees "Ye judge after the flesh, you make rash decisions, but I judge no man. I want you to know that if I judge, my judgement is true for I am not alone, but I and the father that sent me", John 8:15-16.

They thought Jesus was adding salt to injury by calling God his father. They aimed to kill him at the time, and he said "I and my father are one" John 10:30, to which they said that he claimed equality with God.

The Bible advised them that the mind of Christ should be in them, that "Jesus, being in the form of God, thought it not robbery to be equal with God, made himself of no reputation and took upon him the form of a servant, and was made in the likeness of men. Phil. 2:5-7, who put on flesh Jn.1:14.

Because of their attitude to him, he bestowed some woes unto them "Woe unto you, Pharisees, for ye love the uppermost seats in the synagogues and greetings in the market".

"Woe unto you scribes and Pharisees, hypocrites! For ye are as graves which appear not and the men that walk over them are not aware of them".

"Woe unto you Pharisees, for ye tithe mint and rue, and all manners of herbs, and pass over judgement and the love of God; these ought ye to have done, and not to leave the other undone".

The battleground was getting hotter, as he told them that "He that heareth his word and believes in him that sent him, hath everlasting life; and shall not come into condemnation, but is passed from death unto life John 5:19-25. They said that he said they were bound for hell.

At the boiling point, the multitudes went before Jesus with many following, saying "Hosanna to the Son of David; blessed is He that cometh in the name of the Lord, Hosanna in the highest". The Pharisees were jealous, and they could not stomach this.

"What shall we do to this man, see ye how ye prevail nothing? Behold the world is gone after him" John 12:19. They were so bothered, and planned to get hold of him, but his time had not come, and therefore they could not get hold of him.

He got to the temple and cast out all them that sold and bought, and overthrew the tables of the money changers, and the seats of them that sold doves. This upset the Pharisees because most of the hawkers were their agents and Jesus had cut another source of their income. Jesus told them that "My house shall be called the house of prayer; but ye have made it a den of thieves" Mt. 21:9-13.

The Pharisees said among themselves that he had called the temple his house, he had called them thieves, and he had tampered with their income.

They were so concerned about Jesus' miracles that they had to ask him "By what authority did he do these things"? "We know, and acknowledge that it is not the work of man, but tell us what we want to hear that it is your father as usual".

The Philosopher, Socrates, learnt of Jesus by answering questions with questions. Christ told them "I will also ask of you one question, and if you answer me, then I will tell you by what authority I do these things. The baptism of John, was it from heaven, or of men"? "Answer me you hypocrites", he said.

Then they reasoned with themselves, see where he tried to get us stoned by the people, we better not answer this question which is a spiritual one, rather than our own natural questions.

They reasoned that "if we say from heaven, he would ask why we don't believe him, but if we say of men, what would the people do", for John was highly respected and regarded as a Prophet. They thus did not answer the question.

Jesus answered them, "Neither do I tell you by what authority I do these things for you know, but you do not want to acknowledge Mk. 11:27-33.

They were baffled that someone could be cleverer than the whole lot of them combined. They were saying among themselves that it is a wrong saying "that two heads are better than one". In this instance, the heads of all the human beings combined were not nearly as good as the head of Jesus.

They then asked the last question "We know who you are, but the affairs of the world prevent us from acknowledgement. Please, tell us how long doest thou make us to doubt? We see how completely different you are to us all. You seem divine to us; tell us if thou be Christ" John 10:24.

Christ's answer was beyond their imaginations "I told you that I am, and ye believe not. The works I do in my Father's name, they bear witness of me, but you believe not because you are not of my sheep as I said unto you before".

"My sheep hear my voice, and I know them, and they follow me, and I give unto them eternal life, and they shall never perish, neither shall any man pluck them out of my hand".

"My Father, which gave them me is greater than all; and no man, including you Pharisees, that are after me to kill me, are able to pluck them out of my Father's hand. As I told you earlier, I would confirm the truth, I and my Father (God) are one" John 10:30. I wish you know the truth "and the truth, which is myself, shall set you free" John 8: 32.

They tried to stone him, but he escaped from them. Hallelujah.

THE PHARISEES AND THE SABBATH

The Pharisees were observers of days and moons that gave prominence to Sabbath, forgetting the Word of God which says "This is the day which the Lord hath made, we will rejoice and be glad in it" Ps. 118:24.

There was a woman which had a spirit of infirmity eighteen years, and was bowed together, and could in no wise lift herself. The arthritis had almost consumed her.

When Jesus saw her, out of compassion, he called her to him and said unto her "Woman, thou art loose from thine infirmity", and he laid his hands on her; and immediately she was made straight and glorified God.

Then came one of the trouble-shooters, the ruler of the synagogue, who had Sunday to Friday to heal, and could not. He was furious, and jealous, and cried out saying "Can't you keep the Sabbath? You think it is good to do a good thing like this on Sabbath day? Don't you know that there are six days in which men ought to work, and one day to rest. Don't you know that, today being Sabbath, God is resting or asleep on the thone".

The fact is that, God is good all the time, not just six days a week.

The Lord then answered him, and said "Ye hypocrites, doth not each of you on Sabbath loose his ox or ass from the stall, and lead him away to watering? Why don't you let him die of hunger or thirst if you strictly practise Sabbath".

"And ought not this woman, being a daughter of Abraham whom Satan hath bound, lo, these eighteen years be loosed from this bond on the Sabbath day"? Lk. 13: 11-17.

He continued and he said unto them all around "The Son of man is Lord, also of the Sabbath" Lk. 6:5.

And when he had said these things, all his adversaries were ashamed; and all the people rejoiced for all the glorious things that were done by him. Lk. 7:17.

The Pharisees recapitulated all that the Lord had told them, and were wroth to hear that they knew not Abraham, and that he knew Abraham, and that he would be telling lies like them if he said he did not, that he knew him, and keep his saying.

He then said to them "Your Father, Abraham, rejoiced to see my day; and he saw it, and was glad". He saw the day from Paradise where he is, happy that I was coming to save those who hear my word and do it, to deliver them from all of their afflictions; and believe me, that I will give them everlasting life John 3:16.

"Verily, verily, I say unto you, before Abraham was, I am" John 9:56-58.

A snare was laid for you Pharisees, and you were taken. You are not aware, you are found and also caught, because you had striven against me the Lord Jer. 50:24.

In wisdom, in knowledge, and in understanding, Christ Jesus excelled them all. Truly, he is above every thing. Hallelujah.

THE GARDEN KANGAROO COURT

After the Lord had instructed his supper in remembrance of himself, then he went to the Garden of Gethsemane. It had got to be a garden, because man's sin was also manufactured in a garden, i.e. the Garden of Eden.

Man's sin had to be conclusively destroyed in another garden where Jesus could have refused to go on the Calvary Cross.

Having seen that his people had gone into captivity in the Garden of Eden for lack of knowledge, and fallen into disobedience, and hell thus enlarged herself and opened her mouth without measure awaiting all people and that man's glory, and their multitude, and their pomp, and any of them that rejoiceth shall descent into hell Isa. 5:13-14. Christ needed to rectify the situation by shedding his blood for remission of man's sin, and as many that believe in him would be reconciled to God.

He is the good Shepherd who knows his sheep, and his sheep know him; who laid down his life for the sheep. Because of this, the Father loves him, having laid down his life that he might take it again. "No man taketh it from him, but he lay it down of himself. He had power to lay it down and had the power to take it again. That commandment did he receive of his father" John 10:14-18.

He knew that he could pray to his father and receive more than twelve legions of angels to destroy his enemies, but the scriptures must be fulfilled, that he must go on the cross and die there for you and me.

In that garden, Christ prayed so much that his sweat was like drops of blood "Father, if thou be willing, remove the cup from me; that flesh I put on is not willing to undergo crucifixion, nevertheless not my will but thine be done John 1:14.

The Word of God which put on flesh will be willing, so Father, not my will but thine be done. The power of fear was forever broken by Jesus. We therefore need not fear any weapon that Satan throws at us for it shall not prosper Isa. 54:17. Since that day, our spirit is no longer that of fear, but of boldness and power, bringing down Satan's stronghold. 2 Cor 10:4.

An angel appeared unto him from heaven, strengthening him; and there and then settling whether Jesus was going to die or not. Jesus did not say "Father, this type of painful death on the cross does not befit your son", neither did he say "I am not ready or unwilling to bear it".

The Bible says that he did not think along those lines for "he was obedient unto death, even the death of the Cross" Phil. 2:8.

The betrayer, Judas Iscariot, came with soldiers and a multitude to arrest him with swords and staves. Jesus therefore, knowing all things that should come upon him went forth and said to them "Whom seek ye"? And they said "Jesus of Nazareth", and Jesus said to them "I am he", and they went backward and fell to the ground. Truly Christ is above them all. Hallelujah. John 18:6.

Jesus could have gone whilst they were on the ground, but he chose to die for you and me instead.

The devil did not desist. I believe that this was enough for the wise to believe Jesus, but they did not.

Jesus asked them again "Whom seek ye"? They answered him "Jesus of Nazareth". Jesus answered "I have told you, I am He".

One of the disciples smote the servant of the High Priest's right ear, which was cut off. Jesus, as the Prince of Peace said "Suffer ye thus far", and as the Great Physician he touched Malchus' ear and healed him Lk. 22: 49-51.

This healing miracle should have been enough to dissuade them from arresting the Man of Peace, but the contrary was the case. They cared only about arresting Jesus.

Then Jesus surrendered himself and they took him, and led him into the High Priest's house, and Peter followed afar off. All the other disciples had fled.

Although Peter was bold, when promising to die with Jesus, Jesus had told Peter that he would deny him thrice before the cock crowed twice.

I once met a man who said he did not fear death. I said that's fine, but no one except Jesus Christ surrendered himself to it before time; it is natural to fear death.

The man said that, unlike others who fear death, he would stand and face death squarely. Someone then played a trick on him by racing into the room with a sharp knife pretending to be mad, hopping about as if he was going to kill somebody.

The man who didn't fear death ran for his life like everyone else, and felt quite ashamed when he learnt it was a trick on him.

Christ knew that Peter would follow him to the trial and then deny him.

Peter denied Jesus. "As he was beneath the palace, there came one of the maids of the high priest, and when she saw Peter warming himself, she looked upon him and said, and thou also was with Jesus of Nazareth".

But Peter denied, saying "I know not, neither understand I what thou sayest". And he went out into the porch, and the cock crew.

A maid saw him again, and began to say to them that stood by "This is one of them", and he denied it again.

A little after, they that stood by Peter said to him "Surely, thou art one of them, for thou art a Galilean, and thy speech also agreeth thereto". This time, he not only denied but he cursed and swore, saying, "I know not this man of whom ye speak". The cock crew three times, and Christ's prophecy to Peter was fulfilled Mark 14:30.

Peter called to mind the prophecy, and he wept.

THE MOCKED TRIAL

That was the trial that was a complete mockery, and an ungodly act of man in the cruellest trial ever imaginable against our God to fulfil the Scriptures.

"The mouth of the wicked Pharisees, and the mouth of the deceitful Scribes are opened against Jesus; they have spoken against him with a lying tongue.
They compassed him about also with words of hatred, and fought against him without a cause.

For the love of Jesus, they were his adversaries, but he gave himself to prayer "Father, forgive them, for they know not what they do" Lk. 23:34.

"And they have rewarded him evil for good he did, and hatred they showed for his love" Ps. 109 2-5.

In the high priest's house, many atrocities were performed against Jesus. They spat on him, they covered his eyes, beat him, mocked him, all because it was the hour of darkness. "Prophesy now, who is he that smote thee" they said.

All done in the name of salvation. If you have not believed on him that he is the Son of God who came to save you, now is the time for you to do that. The Bible says "For the Lord God will help me; therefore shall I not be confounded, therefore I gave my back to the smiters, and my cheeks to them that plucked off the hair; I hid not my face from shame and spitting; and I do know that I shall not be ashamed said Jesus the Lord Isa. 50:6-7. All this happened at the trial.

The chief priests and all the counsel of the wicked went about saying "They had money to give to false witnesses , those poor people who needed money came to bear false witness against him, but their witness agreed not together, though they took the money.

Then came those who accused him, saying, "We found this fellow perverting the nation, and forbidding to give tribute to Caesar, saying that he himself is Christ a King".

And Pilate asked him, saying, "Art thou the King of the Jews? And Jesus answered him "Thou sayest it".

Then said Pilate to the chief priests, and to the people "I find no fault in this man", i.e. he was innocent.

The crowd, however, were adamant. They wanted to get rid of their maker and God so they said that he stirred up the people, teaching throughout all Jewry, beginning from Galilee to this place.

When Pilate heard of Galilee, he asked whether Jesus were a Galilean, and took the opportunity to transfer him to Herod the king.

Herod was happy to meet Jesus, perhaps a miracle or two he had heard about might now be witnessed. Peradventure, Jesus might just blindfold everyone and vanish!

The Son of God was determined to save us.

Herod questioned Jesus in many words, but Jesus answered him not a single word.

Meanwhile, the chief priests only wish was that Herod should hurry up and let them get on with it.

Herod joined the pack of sinners, mocking Jesus; and he arrayed him in a gorgeous robe and sent him again to Pilate Lk. 23: 1-11.

Pilate stood up and asked Jesus, saying, look at the witnesses, they are bad, false and condemnable. Won't you say something in your defence? But Jesus still held his peace and answered nothing.

They asked "Are you the Son of the Blessed God?"

Then Jesus had to confirm or else be a liar, but thank God he cannot lie Heb. 6:18, so he said emphatically "I Am, and ye shall see the Son of man sitting on the right hand of power, and second time coming in the clouds of heaven Mark 14:62.

Then the high priest rent his clothes (liar and hypocrite he was), and saith "What? Do we need any further witnesses?" "This is all I wanted him to say. You have heard the blasphemy; what think ye? And without much ado, they all condemned him to be guilty of death.

Pilate said to them, "ye have brought this man unto me, as one that perverted the people, and behold, having examined him before your presence, have found no fault in this man, touching those things whereof ye accuse him. To me, he is an innocent man".

"No, nor yet Herod; for I sent you to him, and lo, nothing worthy of death is done unto him. You only want innocent blood on your hand Lk. 23: 13-15. To please you all, I will therefore chastise him, and release him". They cried "Away with this man, and release unto us Bar-ab-bas", who for a certain sedition made in the city and for murder was cast into prison.

Pilate, willing to release Jesus, spoke to them but they cried louder, "Crucify him, Crucify him".

CRUCIFY HIM

Crucify the man who said that we should not make the temple the den of the robbers, who said we are robbers.

Crucify him who deprived us of our gains.

Crucify him who the entire world is about to follow, thus abandoning us.

Crucify him who claimed equality with God as his father John 10:30.

Crucify him who went about doing good, healing those who were oppressed of the devil, delivering all they that the Pharisees did not want released Acts 10:38.

Crucify him who met the people's needs at all times. We want you to know something, and that is that "We just didn't want him around". Phil. 4:19.

Crucify him who cannot be ensnared with all the human tricks, who brought out money from the fish's mouth Mt. 17:24-27.

Crucify him whose wisdom transcends all human wisdom, knowledge and understanding i.e. Caesar's coin.

And he said unto them the third time "Why, what evil hath he done"? "I have found no cause of death in him. I will therefore chastise him and let him go.

The people and chief priests' voices prevailed, and Pilate gave sentence that it should be as they wished. This a political judgement was given, and they led him away, laid hold upon one Simon, a Cyrenian coming out of the country, and on him they laid the cross that he might bear it after Jesus Lk. 23:26-27.

The Bible says that "All we like sheep have gone astray like the chief priests, Pilate, Herod and the mob. We have turned everyone to our ways, and the Lord hath laid on him the iniquity of us all".

He was oppressed, and he was afflicted, yet he opened not his mouth during the mock trial; neither did he defend himself nor blame anyone. He was brought as a lamb to the slaughter, and speechless as a sheep before shearers; he opened not his mouth.

He was taken from prison and from judgement, and who shall declare his generation? For he was cut out off the land of the living; for the transgression of his people was he stricken Isa. 53:6-8.

The Son of God was ready for crucifixion having been lied against Mt. 26: 59-62, having been denied Mk. 14:66-72, having been tortured Mt. 26: 67-68.

Christ, our Passover, was fully ready, and willing to be sacrificed for us.

Therefore, let us keep the feast; not with the old leaven as the Chief Priests, the scribes and the people, neither with the leaven of malice and wickedness; but with the unleavened bread of sincerity and truth 1 Cor 5:7-8, that when we know the truth, we shall be set free, and that the Son of God, Jesus Christ of Nazareth shall set us free. John 8:32-36.

He gave us believers a sound foundation in himself. He said, "I will pray to the father, and he shall give us another Comforter, that he may abide with us forever.

Even the spirit of truth, whom the world cannot receive, because it sees him not, because he is not human with flesh, neither knoweth him, but ye know him; for he dwelleth in us, and shall be in us.

He said that he will not leave us comfortless, he would come to us.

According to his word, he came to us on the day of Pentecost, ten days after his ascension to his throne, and this Comforter gave new tongues to the believers. Hallelujah.

I enjoyed a conversation many years ago when my Muslim brother came to my house and met me praying in tongues. After I finished, my brother said "I tried to copy that language, but I couldn't". I said, if anyone is able to copy the language, that makes it a natural language i.e. a language that could be taught or learnt. I told him that the language is used to defeat Satan and all his demons, I invited him to come to Jesus if he liked it.

The Comforter is now around. Claim him through the one who sent him. Jesus, the Son of the Living God, who surely is above all. John 14: 16-18.

CRUCIFIED FOR DOING GOOD

Christ knew as the Omniscient that his time to leave the world was nigh, he was not frightened, and he was exercising his Divine Authority.

Go unto the city to such a man, and say unto him The Master says "My time to leave this earth is at hand". I will keep the Passover at thy house with my disciples. Mt. 26:18. To that, it was a mixture of joy that the Master chose him as his host, what a great honour? It was sorrowful that his guest sounded a warning that he would soon leave the world, and perhaps see him no more until resurrection day.

The time, as prophesied by Jesus, came. He was arrested and tried by a kangaroo court. The prosecutors had decided on death by crucifixion before they brought Jesus to trial. Though they found it difficult to find witnesses, they went out to bribe people to falsely testify against him. Two hungry paupers said what the elders wanted them to say, and Christ was convicted to death on the cross.

The murderer, Bar-ab-bas was released singing:-

The painful death he should die.
The punishment which befits him
All Jesus has carried away
Thank you Jesus, my Lord
You died because of me

Pilate scoured Jesus, and delivered him to be crucified for doing no wrong.

The soldiers of the governor took him into the common hall, and gathered unto him the whole band of soldiers who stripped him, and put on him a scarlet robe. They plaited a crown of thorns and put it upon his head. They took a reed, put it in his hand, and they bowed their knee as they will on judgement day. They mocked him, which they will not be able to do on that day.

The Bible says that when the great day of his wrath is come; who shall be able to stand? Rev 6:17. By the way, the crown of thorns changed to many crowns on his head with gold, diamonds, emeralds etc.

Their song of "Hail the King of the Jews" will be changed to Amen, amen, blessings and glory Rev. 7:12.

Christ said "Woe unto them that laughed, for they shall mourn and weep" Luke 6:25.

They spat upon him, and took the reed and smote him on the head, and after they had mocked him, they took the robe off from him and put his won raiment upon him and led him away to crucify him, ranting "crucify him, crucify him" Mk. 15:19.

All have sinned and come short of the Glory of God Rom. 3:23. They were all wicked men, driven away in their wickedness. They all sinned against him and wronged their own souls. They all hated Jesus and reaped eternal separation from God forever as they loved death Prov. 8:36. Christ, however, forgave them for they did not know what they were doing.

They led him to Golgotha "The place of the skull", tied him to the cross, and there, God took his eyes away from his son because God is of purer eyes than to behold the atrocities performed on his son. He could not look at the sins, iniquities and transgressions of the entire world that Jesus was carrying on the cross. "Therefore, he lookest upon them that deal treacherously, and held his tongue when those wicked men devoured Jesus, the Righteous One" Hab. 1:13.

There were two thieves crucified with him on the cross, and though they were in pain, they had their own comments. The first thief on his left said "If thou be Christ then save thyself and save us". He was seeking a fake salvation to enable him to continue in his crime; but the thief on the right hand rebuked his partner in crime, saying "Don't you fear God? This man Jesus is not a criminal as ourselves". He reminded his partner that they deserved all the punishment meted on them; but Jesus was an innocent man, dying for the guilty.

In pain, this man cried out "Jesus remember me in your kingdom". The answer and the promise of the Lord to him was "Verily, I say unto thee, today shalt thou be with me in paradise". Lk. 23:43.

The people passing by were not found wanting in their revellings "If thou be the Son of God, do not complete the work of salvation, come down from the cross". To the chief priests, Jesus was in the tightest corner, there was no hiding place. "You saved others, yourself you cannot save, obey Satan's plan & come down from the cross if thou be the King of Israel".

They failed to believe that God could save any one he wishes to save, saying "Jesus, you trusted God, let him deliver you now. This is the time you need the one you call your father" Matt. 27:43. They heard Jesus with the word of assurance of salvation, as he did not count all their sins against them; by forgiving them and asking his father also to forgive them for they know not what they do. They were very cruel ignorants who needed nothing more than forgiveness Lk. 23:34.

God's reply was "You came as their Redeemer & Saviour, if you forgive them, I do as well".

Jesus saw his mother, and the disciple he loved standing helplessly by, and said unto his mother "Woman, behold thy son", and he said to his disciple "Behold thy mother". Obviously, Mary's husband must have been dead for him to send his mother to be taken care of the disciples, and not by her husband; "Whatever God has joined together, let no man put asunder" Mt. 19:6.

The Book of Psalms say "God has known Christ's reproach and his shame, and his dishonour; how the people have reproached him, how they did not give honour to him who honour is due, how they boldly reproached him face to face, how it broke his heart and there was no comforter to comfort him" Psalm 69:19-21.

In answer to his plea "I thirst", they gave him gall and vinegar to drink Jn. 19:28-29. There was an inscription on his head "King of the Jews", which did not tally with his title as "King of Kings and Lord of Lords".

When it was time, he said "It is finished", and he gave up the ghost. When beggars die, there are no comets seen, but the heavens themselves blaze forth the death of Princes. As soon as Christ said it is finished:-

Darkness covered the entire land.
The day became night.
The earth quaked.
The sun and moon bowed down to the Son of God.
The veil of the temple was rent in twain.

Then a direct way of truth and life opened to anyone who seeks God through Jesus Christ, the Son of God, the Sun of Righteousness, who would arise from his throne above with healing in his wings, then we can go forth and grow up as calves of the stall Mal. 4:2.

IT IS FINISHED

A strong consolation came to all who have fled for refuge, to lay hold upon Jesus Christ who is set before us, the hope and anchor of our soul, sure and steadfast as he entered within the veil.

Our High Priest who alone forever offered himself as a Living Sacrifice, who is consecrated for us, through the breaking down of the partition between God and man, suffered for us by shedding his blood and thereby brought to us a new and profitable living way; by boldly entering into the holiest by his Blood.

No more vain oblations are acceptable to God, who said that he would take no bullock out of thy house, nor he-goats out of they folds. For every beast of the forest is his, and the cattle upon a thousand hills belong to him. All the fowls of the mountains, and the wild beasts of the field belong to him. He says that he will not eat the flesh of bulls, nor drink the blood of goats. Psalm 50: 9-13. The Lord accepteth them not, and he will remember their iniquity and visit their sins. They shall go into bondage Hos. 8:13. because the everlasting unshakeable foundation laid for us all, which is Christ Jesus, is rejected by them and fail they to heed the Word of God, that "Neither is there salvation in any other; for there is none other name under heaven given among men, whereby we must be saved Acts 4:12.

We must all look unto Jesus whose blood cleans us from all sins, and from all unrighteousness 1 Jn. 1:7,9.

Through Jesus, the salvation of man is signed, sealed and delivered, and to go outside him is vanity. It is written, "O ye sons of men, how long will ye love vanity and seek after the Lord?" But know he that hath set apart Christ Jesus for himself, and will hear when you call him through the name of Jesus Psalms 4:2-3.

If you believe that he died and shed his blood, then you can plead it and you will surely be out of Satan's claws, and then you will overcome all the power of darkness, and be translated into the kingdom of Jesus the dear Son of God; much as redemption through his blood awaits you through his precious blood, your sins shall also be forgiven, written unto Christ's account Col. 1:13-14.

His death opened the door to the Father, no more need of an intermediary to plead for you. The name of Jesus is the key, as the author of eternal salvation unto all that obey him. It is now needless to struggle on your own for, as soon as you cast your cares upon him, he will take them up as he cares so much for you.

Concerning your health, Christ has World Health Supernatural Service. He is the great physician who heals when others fail, whose prescription is the stripes he received in the hands of the soldiers before his crucifixion 1 Ptr. 2:24.

In Christ, the time of poverty is gone, ended. There will be no more hunger, no more wants, for "God shall supply all your needs according to his riches in glory by Christ Jesus". O taste and see that the Lord is good. You shall be blessed if you trust him, for there is no want to them that fear him. There will be no lack as the young lions do lack and suffer hunger. Remember that they that seek Jesus the Lord shall not want any good thing because they are with them when asking. Psalm 34: 8-10.

Today, the ugly face of fear might be threatening you. The one thing to remember is that there is an eternal purpose in Christ.

Jesus, our Lord in whom we have boldness and access with confidence by the faith of him, therefore faint not at any tribulations. Eph. 3:11-13.

It is finished. There is no more Jews, nor Gentiles. All in Christ are made one. He is our peace and he has broken down the middle wall of partition between us.

Having abolished in his flesh, the enmity, even the law of commandments contained in ordinances, for to make in himself of two things, one new man, so making peace. He had through his death slain the enemy, which is the laws of commandments "Eph 2:15-16".

Begging the devil is over. You can have full enjoyment of power and full anointing of the Holy Ghost Acts 1:4-8. Cast the devil out in Jesus name.

It is finished, the fear of the curse of the law is wiped clean for Christ has been made a curse for us. It is written, "Cursed is everyone that hangs on a tree". His hanging brought the blessing of Abraham on the Gentiles, that they might receive the promise of the Holy Spirit through faith Gal. 3:13-14.

The Old Covenant is wiped out clean, finished with, and the sealing of the New Covenant is made with the Blood of Jesus which blots out the handwriting of ordinances that was against us, which was contrary to us. He took it out of the way, nailed it to his cross. No more sin offerings needed, for he is above offerings. He was offered once and for all.

"And having spoiled principalities and powers, he made a show of them openly, triumphing over them in it". Therefore, principalities and whatever powers should not frighten you, nor are they in a position to overcome you for our Master Jesus is above them all. Col. 2:14-15.

It is finished, no more insurmountable mountains, for we can do all things through Jesus who strengthens us Phil. 4:13.

We can just face any weapons of the enemy for "In Christ, no weapon that is formed against us shall prosper, that we shall put into condemnation every tongue wagged against us since the righteousness of Jesus is our righteousness" Isa. 54:17.

Part of the benefit of Christ's completion of his assignment is that "There shall no evil be able to touch us" Job 5:19.

As apples of God's eyes, his protection is assured Zech. 2:8, being surrounded by the angels of the Lord.

In his blood is prosperity. It was promised to us that the God of heaven will prosper us. Neh. 2:20.

That whatsoever we do shall not fail, but prosper. Ps. 1:3.

That we shall not die prematurely, but live and declare the works of the Lord Ps. 118:17.

That the Lord is the shield of our help. Dt. 33:29.

God had raised his Son, having loosed the pains of death; because it was not possible that he should be holden of it. Acts 2:24.

I do not know if you have witnessed people dying before. To the unbelievers, there is much pain, the pang of death is terrible, and the gripe is honestly unbelievable.

I have witnessed someone dying before, and I don't understand why it is called the cold hand of death, and I felt as terrible as the sick person ready to die. The pain and all the incoherent language by the one ready to die made me realise that only Christ at someone's death bed can overcome the melancholy and ache of dying.

The worst for the unbeliever is that there is an everlasting punishment worse than the pain described. Where the unbeliever goes, there will be panic, chaos, and no end in sight.

On getting there, the unbeliever will be met with the inscription "This is not a place of rest, joy or hope". Do not think in that line "a pity they missed heaven". It will, at first be like a dream, but alas it won't have an end, but will be everlasting torment.

I am not an apostle of woe, but an apostle of truth, and the above is not an exaggeration. I have seen hell, and thank God it was only for three minutes.

There was a man who was really religious. He became sick and could not eat for days. He was reeling in pain so much that many around him were crying even before his demise. Someone asked him why he could not taste even water. He answered "can't you see the cock pecking my feet". We saw nothing but, spiritually, he was a wreck even though he was the leader of his religion with a big title.

But of truth, Christ bears the pain of death for us. A lady from church rang me to say that her mother was sick, and asking for tea. She asked me to pray for her, which I did.

Less than 30 minutes later, the daughter rang back to say that her mother was dead. She said that her mother's last words had been "Jesus, Jesus, let me in", and just after that, she went to be with the Lord.

What is the difference between these two deaths? It is that Jesus has swallowed up death in victory, the rebuke of death he took away from his people. From off all the earth, a meaningful rebuke is taken away by Jesus, for precious in the sight of the Lord is the death of his saints. "Therefore, he loosed the bonds of death off his followers" Ps. 116: 15-16.

It is written that "The wages of sin is death, but the gift of God is through life through Jesus Christ" Rom. 6:23.

The wages of not accepting Jesus Christ is painful death, when one is to leave this world. The gift of God is ending up in a place of joy, happiness, and everything that is good.

I invite you to Jesus who holds the keys of death and hell which he seized in the grave. No one else but him alone is able to say "I am he that liveth, and was dead; and behold, I am alive for ever more, and have the keys of hell and of death". Rev. 1:18.

As awful as death may seem, as gruesome and calamitous hell is, they both have a Master who will cast both of them into the lake of fire Rev. 20:14. Give it a serious thought for the choice between a joyful death which leads to eternal life with Jesus, and a painful death with all its woes, that ends up with Satan in hell are laid before everyone today. The choice is yours alone, and may the Lord help you all to make a rightful choice.

CRUCIFIED FOR DOING GOOD

This had to happen for it was on the Calvary cross that the power of sin was totally destroyed. Jesus carried all the known and the unknown sins mentioned in 1 Cor. 6:9-10, Gal. 5:19-21, and all that were mentioned everywhere else in the Bible, to the cross.

That time, Jesus Christ the Righteous One 1 John 2:1 took our place and wiped clean all sins confessed and repented. We are righteous because he had been made sin for us 2 Cor. 5:21, and without a shred of doubt, we that are made righteous by him shall shine forth as the sun on the kingdom of our father.

Many today think that the Cross is a figment of imagination, but it is not. The forerunner, John the Baptist said that "as many as received him as the Son of God, who went to the Cross and died there, and resurrected the third day with Jesus, to them he gave power to become the sons of God, even to them that believe on his name as Christ the Saviour" John 1:12.

We are crucified with him, nevertheless live, yet not us, but Christ liveth in us the life we now live in the flesh. We live by faith on the Son of God who loved us, and gave himself for us. His going to the cross was not in vain Gal. 2:20.

LORD OVER THE GRAVE

The Book of Eccle. 6:3 says that "if a man begat 100 children, and live many years, so that the days of his years be many; and his soul be not filled with good, also that he have no burial; I say that an untimely birth (miscarriage) is better than he.

The Pharisees and company, who thought that they had, seen the end of Jesus; those that said he was a fake that "could anything good come out of Nazareth", had only one aim. That was, to know who would care to bury him, so as to mark such a person out for possible future arrest. They wanted Jesus to be buried like an ass, drawn and cast forth beyond the gates of Jerusalem Jer. 22:19.

Because of fright, no relative of Jesus came for his body; his faithful disciples had deserted him, even the boldest among them denied him three times. It was a very hard and troubled time for them all.
When the evening was come, because money talks, a rich man named Joseph of Arimathea, who was a disciple of Jesus, went to Pilate and begged for the body of Jesus.

Pilate, who loved money, obliged Joseph.

Nichodemus, who was a ruler of the Jews, and a teacher in Israel, came out boldly and joined Joseph in Christ's funeral. They took the body down from the Cross, and wrapped it in linen having embalmed it with a mixture of myrrh, and aloes about hundred pounds in weight, and having added spices as was the manner of the Jews.

Nichodemus had once spoken in defence of Jesus within the Council. Although a ruler, he was a just and pious man who did not have a hand in the counsel of the wicked that condemned Jesus. He was obviously opposed to his colleagues. He became a secret believer when advised to be born again by the Lord, no doubt that he found a way to defend Jesus.

Out of love and compassion, not minding what his colleagues would say, he came out openly to join Joseph to bury Jesus. They had once asked him if he also was of Galilee, but after burial it would be Nichodemus. "Thou surely art half Galilean, if not full-blooded, and we can confirm undoubtedly that you are his disciple".

Whatever they said in addition to this stuck for only two days because, on the third day, Nichodemus had the last laugh, and laughed best. He was able to say to the Council "You can see now that the man, Jesus, crucified by you out of jealousy is the Son of God as he said. I can of myself confirm my secret meeting with him, as he said I must be born again. I can tell you that no man ever spoke as him.

The rest of the episode is a conjecture for anyone to see. He really laughed them to scorn.

Both Joseph of Arimathea, and Nichodemus in the presence of the soldiers laid Christ's body in the new tomb hewn out in the rock; and with the help of the soldiers they rolled a great stone to the door of the sepulchre, and both men left for their homes.

Getting rid of Jesus was the greatest joy to the elders. They called the Lord a deceiver and liar as themselves. They were liars who did not confess that Jesus came in the flesh. They were deceivers, and surely anti-christ 2 John 7.

The priests and Pharisees went jubilantly to inform Pilate that Christ had boasted that he would come out of the grave the third day, but they believed that it was only a trick, that his disciples would come and steal his body Mt. 27:63.

"Command therefore, that the sepulchre be made safe and secure, to stop his disciples from coming at night to steal his body, and say that he is risen from the dead; so that the last error of not making sure that he remained in his grave for ever shall be worse than killing him.

Pilate who in anger knew that he gave a human unrighteous judgement said "You have a watch, go your way, make it sure as you can". The soldiers tried all human methods, they sealed the stone and then they left some soldiers as guards at the tomb on a night and day vigil with prayers. They were all satisfied, including the chief priests, that not a fly could come near the sepulchre. They made sure that it was the guards who hated Jesus that were on duty. Those who were prominent in shouting "Crucify him".

Be it known to you today, that they did make sure that nobody dared attempt coming near there. The area became "Out of bounds".

Jesus Christ made his grave with the wicked and the rich, a righteous man with no sin, neither wicked nor unruly. For it pleased God to bruise him Isa. 53:10. He went into the grave amidst joy by his arch enemies. This was a pre-ordained plan of God that the grave might be defeated, that the redemption of human sins should be accomplished. He was there, and his flesh rested in hope for he knew that his father would not leave his soul in hell, neither would he see corruption, for the grave could in no way hold him captive. He was saying "O grave, I will be thy destruction" Hos. 13;14, thus death and the grave became powerless. O death, where is thy sting? O grave, where is thy power? He scraped the grave of its victory over man, and handed it to us making us victorious, overcomers, and more than conquerors Rom. 8:37.

The grave's desire was for him to be laid like a sheep in it, but he was not because he was Lord. Even in the grave, he gave the message of redemption to those in captivity; unlike most of the people of today, many in the grave accepted the message and became saints that came out after Christ's resurrection. Mt 27:52.

The grave was discomfited, as it happened that the third day, the Son of God, Jesus Christ of Nazareth came out of it. The devil and his hosts holding a party were baffled and fled the party.

Now the Father, having welcomed him home, set him on his right hand in the heavenly places, far above principalities and powers and might, and dominion, and far above every name that is named Buddha, Confucius, Socrates, Mohammed, Pastors, Pope, Moses, Elijah, your name and my name. His name is far above those of the archangels Michael, Gabriel and Satan with all his demons.

The angels in heaven do worship him every minute and every second. We too must extol him who is our God, the King of Kings. We must bless his Holy Name for ever and ever, for we shall be with him for ever and ever. Great is the Lord of lords, and greatly to be praised, and his greatness is unsearchable.

The Bible says that he did no sin, neither was guile found in his mouth. Yet, he was brutalised, suffered horrendously, went into the grave, relied on his father who judgeth not as man. That, having carried our sins to the cross, and having went into the grave, would elevate him who carried all our sins in his own body, and nailed it to the cross; so that we that are soaked in sins should have forgiveness through his righteousness, and be healed by the thirty-nine stripes he received 1 Ptr. 2:22-24.

We must not forget that it was upon the Son of God, found in fashion as a man, that all these atrocities were performed.

He succumbed to the most brutal death, even the death on the cross. This obedience brought magnanimity such that the Father gave him a name which is above every name that "At the name of Jesus, every knee should bow, and invisible things under the earth like the dead, should be subject to Christ's authority".

Every one that has a mouth to speak should confess that "Jesus Christ is Lord to the glory of the Father" Phil. 2:8-10.

His visit to the grave, and resurrection from it brought glory, honour and power to the Son of God who gives glory and honour to his Father.

His going to the grave, and coming out of it alive brings confidence that we have a High Priest who has authority over life, death and the grave; we have an assurance that he who defeated death and the grave will fulfil his promise to raise us up at the last day; that every one that believeth on him will live everlasting, for he is alive for ever more Rev. 1:8.

He conquered the grave, for he is that, who cometh from above, and he is above all things. Remember that the grave could not hold him into captivity. He is the Lord above the power of the grave.

Finally, the dead, small and great will stand before him. The books shall be opened, which is the book of life, and the dead including the Pharisees and Chief Priest, and all anti-christs will be judged out of those things which were written in the books, according to their works.

The sea will give up the dead, which were in them, and death and hell (grave) will deliver up the dead to be judged by Christ who destroyed both death and the grave, and cast them both into the lake of fire. Rev. 20:12-14.

I AM THE RESURRECTION

The Lord Jesus Christ, who was above death, through resurrection said when he was to raise Lazarus that "He is the resurrection and the life; he that believeth in me, though he were dead, yet shall he live".

And whosoever liveth, and believeth in me shall never die. Believe you this"? John 11:25-26.

He demonstrated resurrection power here to the highest, as he raised Lazarus a four day dead body from his grave. We should know that man being body, soul and spirit, only looses the corruptible body to the ground, but the soul and spirit to paradise and God respectively. God can call them both to join together with the incorruptible body.

He demonstrated resurrection to show that he and no one else created the humans John 1:1-3. He that raised the dead, can he too not resurrect? He died to visit the dead in captivity.

Jesus had to be there for those three days to preach unto the spirits in prison, that they might be judged according to men in the flesh, but live according to God in the Spirit. 1 Peter 3:9, 4:6.

This answers the question "What happened to the dead before Jesus visited the world". The dead heard the message that God so loved the world that He gave his only begotten son that whosoever believeth in him should not perish but have everlasting life" John. 3:16, when he went there.

It was the message that "whosoever believeth", and as we see in the Bible, that many believed and became the Saints that came out of the grave to visit the city after Christ's resurrection. Matt. 27:52-53. Abraham, Isaac, Jacob, the old saints, the new saints i.e. the dead that believed bear witness that Jesus is Lord.

Christ confirmed his authority over everybody. He said "truly, truly, the hour is coming and the time is now, that the dead shall hear the voice of the Son of God; and they that hear the voice as the Saints in the grave shall live. We are not dead, we must hear him" Mk. 9:7.

He has life in himself, just as the Father has, and the Father had given him authority to judge. No one should be surprised that the time is imminent when all the dead shall hear Christ's voice. "And all shall resurrect either the resurrection of life, or those that rely on themselves to save themselves, that don't believe in the Name of Jesus unto the resurrection of damnation" John 5:25-29.

When the Saints in the graves came out, the whole of the Holy City was shaken. People asked one another "did any of your dead relatives visit you when Jesus Christ arose?" The dead told the living that the graves had a "Greater than itself visitor", who is above the grave, and who is the Son of God. Even the controller of the grave, Satan, believed and trembled James 2:19.

The devil believed, but he encouraged the chief priests and company to suppress the truth. However, as usual, he failed. The scoffers jesting about the resurrection were put into open shame. Everybody knew that Christ came out of the grave, destroyed the power of the devil, and gave the victory to us; making us victorious, overcomers, and more than conquerors for he loved us Rom. 8:37.

I heartily sing the song "My soul magnifies the Lord, and my spirit praise his name. For even death could not hold him captive, even in the grave, Jesus is Lord. Psalm 16: 8-10.

OUR GOD IS A GOD OF MIRACLES

As a Muslim for over forty seven years, I used to think that Pastors are mere magicians.

I did not know that God anointed him mightily through his son Jesus, until I too became a tool for Jesus.

Our Jesus, who is above all, will always continue to do his miracles as He is the same yesterday, today, and forever Heb. 13:8.

There was a man with severe hypertension who constantly sweated, and said that the blood was running inside his legs and arms. They said he had a heart problem.

Doctors prescribed all sorts of drugs for him to no avail, but when he was brought to our church, Jesus Christ the perfect Healer healed him.

I went to Sokoto, a Muslim state in Nigeria where I met a man who was possessed by the devil. I reminded Jesus of the mad man of the Gardarene, and Jesus Christ healed the man.

A blind woman in Ibadan in Nigeria was touched by the Lord as I lay my hand on her. God restored the one blind eye. Don't ask me how? It was just by the Word which says that "These signs shall follow them that believe; in Christ's name shall they cast out devils, they shall speak with new tongues, they shall lay hands on the sick and they shall recover Mk. 16:17-18.

In a deliverance service, again in Ibadan, many witches were arrested by the Power of Jesus, shouting and slayed under the anointing of the Holy Spirit they confessed Jesus as Lord.

This meeting was of a difference in that one of these witches failed to come out, but immediately after the service she felt unable to go out of the church, she was unable to sit down, but just walked round and round in circles.

One of the Pastors told her the church was to be locked up then she told the Pastor what had happened. I went to pray for her as the Spirit led, and soon she was manifesting and went down under the Holy Spirit.

Because her husband was a Muslim, and not in church, he came to look for his wife. He met his wife on the ground with six of us praying over her. The husband waited for one hour and the following week, the whole family came to church.

A man who had a swollen liver was healed.

He had wanted to borrow some money to pay a herbalist. I told him to come to the Deliverance Service, which he did. He came to meet Jesus. After laying down on the floor for 2 hours, he got up and said that he saw a very tall man with a whiter than white long robe, who asked him if he knew Jesus.

He answered Jesus "Yes", but Jesus said "No", and that he should get to know him.

The man's belly receded the next day, and he was able to drive his car that he had abandoned for quite a while.

This man did not return to church, but said that he was the secretary of a church where they did not believe in healing.

Our God is a universal God. In London, a woman bedevilled by miscarriages came to our church. When she became pregnant, we bound the spirit of miscarriages and she gave birth to a healthy boy.

Christ covers all things. By His stripes we are healed.

A lady was told to come to hospital for an operation on a hole in her heart. I asked her to pray with me, and when she did she went back to hospital and no hole was found, because Jesus had blocked up the hole.

Still in the church, a wealthy woman slept in the afternoon. When she woke up, she found things written on her palm. She tried to wash it away with soap etc, but the writing would not go.

She then came to my house. I was happy she had come because, before this, no one could preach to her.

She asked me to try to wash it off, but nothing could wash away what Satan had written on her palm. I prayed a prayer of faith with her, and pleaded the Blood of Jesus on what was written. The lady remains in church today, because Jesus washed away the words of the devil with his blood.

There are many more miracles and testimonies happening in the House of God, and all praise be to Jesus whose name is above all diseases and impediments. It is written that "the young lions do lack and suffer hunger; but they that seek the Lord shall not want anything good".

Whatever is your problem, I say, take them to Jesus. He is obviously above your problems. He is waiting today. He said "Come to me all ye that labour and are heavy laden, and I will give you rest. Take my yoke upon you, and learn of me; for I am meek and lowly in heart, and ye shall find rest unto your souls. For my yoke is easy, and my burden is light" Mt. 11:28-30.

Know of a fact, that Jesus Christ is above all situations. Hallelujah.

HIS BLOOD IS FLOWING

The Blood of Jesus is not crying vengeance. It is crying salvation. "For the Lord takes pleasure in his people; he will beautify the meek with salvation as the wells of salvation shall spring forth with great deliverance, and terror will not come near his people. In righteousness shalt thou be established; thou shalt be far from oppression; for thou shalt not fear; and from terror; for it shall not come near thee. Isa. 54:14.

The blood of Jesus is crying "Blessings", saying "In blessing I will bless thee, and in multiplying, I will multiply thee, and thy seed shall possess the gate of his enemies Gen. 22:17.

"He shall be like a tree planted by the rivers of water, that bringeth forth his fruit in his season; and whatsoever he doeth shall prosper".

His precious blood is crying "Peace". "Peace I leave with you, my peace I give unto you; not as the world giveth, give I unto you. Let not your heart be troubled, neither let it be afraid" John 14:27.

The blood's assurance is "Freedom", saying "I will undo the burdens, and to let the oppressed go free, and will break every yoke; for if the Son shall set you free, you shall be free indeed John 8:36.

I will come and heal you Mt. 8:7. There is redemption though this blood, and the forgiveness of your sins are awaiting anyone that comes to Jesus. "Come unto me, all ye that labour and are heavy laden, and I will give you rest". Eph 1:7, Mt. 11:28

HIS BLOOD IS FLOWING

The Lord God said "For the life of the flesh is in the blood. There is no life in anyone without blood. The flesh is dead as soon as the blood is not functioning in the body. God requires it on the altar for the atonement of souls.

It is that part of the body which is alive even after death. God told Cain who killed his brother Abel "What hast thou done? The voice of thy brother's blood crieth unto me from the ground" Gen 4:10. Blood is not a part of the body that dies.

Even when God required the blood of animals, He commanded the people to offer lambs without blemish; a male of the first year whose blood they must strike on the two side posts and on the upper door post of the house, i.e. the blood of Jesus in your heart and soul, to change you into the temple of the living God 2 Cor. 6:16. It must not be eaten.

The soldiers that came to Jesus saw that he was dead already, and they broke not his legs, but one of them with a spear pierced his side and forthwith came out of there blood and water; to fulfil the word which said "And I will pour upon the house of David, and upon the inhabitants of Jerusalem the Spirit of grace and of supplications; and they shall look upon me "whom they have pierced", and they shall mourn for me as one mourneth for his only son, and shall be in bitterness for me, as one that is in bitterness for his firstborn.

In that day shall there be a great mourning of Hadadrimom-mon in the Valley of Megid-don, and every family shall mourn Zech. 12:10-14. John 19:34.

No wonder the whole of the land mourned. When the day became night, and the veil was rent in the midst. People knew that something out of the ordinary did happen, that an innocent blood had been shed, the Son of God was crucified, the sun and moon bowed down Lk. 23:45.

The Lord completed his mission to establish the New Testament with his blood, which he shed for many, not for all, but for anyone that believes him as Lord and Saviour, and the Son of God will be included among the many. Whosoever is purchased with the blood becomes the Child of God, and are led by the Spirit of God John 1:12.

Jesus is he whom God has set forth to be propitiation through faith in his blood, to declare his righteousness for the remission of sins, that are past through the mercy of God.

As we are now justified by his blood, we shall be saved from wrath through him, for it if when we were enemies we were reconciled to God by the death of his Son, how much more being reconciled shall we be saved by his life. We also joy in God through our Lord Jesus Christ, by whom we now received the atonement (forgiveness) of sins. Rom. 5:9-11.

The blood has given us a tremendous advantage over those who do not see the light as well as those who see, but are not in the light. While we have redemption through his blood, the forgiveness of sins, according to the riches of his grace, they are missing the grace of God.

The blood of goats, rams, or turtledoves cannot redeem anyone. God does not look at any other blood, besides the Blood of his Son which was shed for us. "For God so loved the world that He gave his only begotten Son, that whosoever believeth in him should not perish, but have everlasting life" John 3:16.

The Word of God says "Hear ye rulers of Sodom; give ear unto the law of our God, ye people of Gomor-rah who relied upon the blood of animals, saying the blood had washed them clean". God rejected their offerings of blood. "To what purpose is the multitude of your sacrifices unto me", saith the Lord; "I am full of the burnt offerings of rams, and the fat of fed beasts; and I delight not in the blood of bullocks of burnt offerings, or of lambs, or of the goats". He says that all these are not required at your hand. To come to His presence, all these are vain oblations.

If you substitute the blood of animals to attract Jesus attention, even the new moons celebrated by the ignorants, and the Sabbaths, the calling of the assemblies; our God cannot bear. It is all iniquity. Psalm 40:6, Isa. 1:10-14.

God's soul hateth, and are all troubles unto Him. He is troubled, wearied to bear them. He is saying that annual ram slaughter, worshipping of celestial or cherubim hosts he hates. They are abominations, and sins of which the wages is death Rom. 6:23a.

Today, however, though the wages of sin is death; there is hope in that "The gift of God is eternal life through Jesus Christ our Lord" Rom. 6:23 (b).

Have you put yourself on the scale? The blood, being the life in man, must not be shed so murderers will not inherit the Kingdom of God, for whosoever sheddeth man's blood, by man shall his blood be shed. For in the image of God made he man Gen. 9:6. However, to make the blood of Jesus shed on that Calvary cross a propitiation for our sins, Christ on the Calvary cross cried "Father, forgive them, for they know not what they do" Lk. 23:34.

Today, that blood whispers "peace, perfect peace". In this great world of sin, the blood of Jesus whispers peace, calling you all that labour and are heavy laden.

It will bring peace of mind unto your soul as you are reading this book. It is the blood of protection. It is the blood that the devil sees, and believes, and he trembles. James 2:19.

The importance of the blood was stretched by the Lord Jesus in person as he was eating with the disciples. He took bread, and bless it, and brake it, and gave it to the disciples, and said "Take, eat, this is my body".

And he took the cup, and gave thanks, and gave it to them saying "Drink ye, all of it, for this is my blood of the New Testament (abrogating the Old Testament) which is shed for many for the remission of sins" Mt. 26:26-28.

Verily, verily, I say unto you "Except ye eat the flesh of the Son of Man, and drink his blood, ye have no life in you".

"Whosoever eateth my flesh, and drinketh my blood, hath eternal life; and I will raise him up at the last day. For my flesh is meat indeed, and my blood is drink indeed. He that eateth my flesh, and drinketh my blood dwelleth in me, and I in him".

"As the living Father hath sent me, and I live by the Father; so he that eateth me, even he shall live by me".

"This is that bread which came down from heaven, not as your fathers did eat man-na, and are dead. He that eats this bread shall live for ever" John 6:53-58.

Paul, writing on the perfection of Christ's sacrifice through his blood said that Jesus became a High Priest of good things to come, by a greater and more perfect tabernacle, the Holy Spirit, not made with hands. That is to say, not of the ordinary building, but by the Holy Ghost living in the believers.

The good things do not come by the blood of goats and calves, but by his own blood with which he entered in once into the holy place, and thereby obtained priceless eternal redemption for us.

The blood of bulls, and of goats, and the ashes of the burnt heifer did sanctify to the purifying of the flesh, thereby people were not delivered from sins, and were unable to serve the Living God in truth and in spirit.

Now Christ is the Mediator of the New Testament, that by means of death, for the redemption of the transgressions that were under the first testament, everyone that answers his calling will receive the promise of eternal inheritance through his death, which did happen. Where a testament is, there must be a testator, and the inheritors could not inherit until after the testator's demise.

The first testament was dedicated with blood of calves, and of goats, with water and scarlet wool, and hyssop, and sprinkled both the book and all the people saying "This is the blood of the testament which God had enjoined unto you".

He then sprinkled with blood both the tabernacle, and all the vessels of the ministry, and almost all things are by the law purged with blood; and without the shedding of blood there is no remission Heb. 9:22.

All that Moses did was earthly, when Christ came, the heavenly, which are better sacrifices came with him.

For Christ did not enter into the holy places made with hands which are earthly; but he entered into the heavenly itself, now in the presence of God pleading for us permanently - not yearly, but perpetually. He had put away the law of sin, nailed it to the cross by the sacrifice of himself. His blood is still flowing and saying "The painful death we should have suffered. The punishment for sin, we should have endured, All he had carried away".

Now come unto me, or why should you perish, all ye that labour and are heavy laden, and I will give you rest.

Take my yoke upon you, and learn of me; for I am meek and lowly in heart, and ye shall find rest unto your souls. For my yoke is easy, and my burden is light Mt. 11:28-30.

Look at the blood flowing, you need not suffer as it is written and appointed unto men once to die, but after this the judgement.

Christ said, "look at the blood flowing, I had been offered to bear the sins of many, and if you look for me, I shall appear the second time without sin unto salvation; for there is now no condemnation to them which are in me, who walk not after the flesh, but after the spirit".

Know that the law of the Spirit of life in Me hath set you free from the law of sin and of death Rom. 8:1-2. If you therefore look for him, he said he shall appear unto you the second time without sin unto salvation, you will find yourself in peace.

Now the God of peace that brought again from the dead our Lord Jesus, that great Shepherd of the sheep, through the blood of the everlasting covenant, make you perfect in every good work to do his will and to be working in you, that which is well-pleasing in his sight through Jesus Christ, to whom be glory for ever and ever Heb. 13: 20-21.

I will ask you to say it loud and clear with me, that the blood of Jesus which purchased me shall never be stained, it is flowing sweeter than milk and honey.

The perfect blood of Jesus which purchased me shall never be stained, for it is the blood ordained of God.

It can never, never be stained.

I say that may you also be one of those who will come out of the great tribulation, and have washed their robes, and make them white in the blood of the Lamb when he comes the second time. Rev. 7:14.

WHETHER THE DEVIL LIKES IT OR NOT

We have heard umpteen times that Christ is coming again but, to many, it is impossible. He said it, I believe it, and wish above all things that you too believe it.

Many will be wondering, when is he coming? Why is he not staying where he is in heaven? Why can't he leave them alone in this place of woe they now live?

Many things happened to him because of you when he came to this sinful world about two thousand years ago.

If you would like to know whether what he said about coming again is true, look in the Bible and see what the Lord Jesus said in Matthew 24 on the signs of his coming, which is imminent. "He warned everyone to take heed that no man deceive you that he shall not come".

It may seem a long time that you have been hearing it, but God does not count time as we do "For a thousand years in his sight are but as yesterday, when it is past, and as a watch in the night, i.e. at best. Twelve hours of our time, i.e. our own one day, is 2000 years of God Ps. 90:4.

In Mt. 24, he said "Many shall come in his name". We have seen many false prophets.

One in Nigeria married thirty eight wives, and had many concubines. When asked why he said that he took "pity on these women and their daughters"; never the pity on their sons.

There are rumours of wars, you can hardly see a Continent in the world where rumours of wars are not raging. Nations against nations, kingdoms against kingdom, Famines and pestilence; all you need as proof is to watch the news on the television, and you see human suffering and deprivation.

"Then shall they deliver you up to be afflicted". It took my mother four years to come to my house after I converted from the Islam religion. However, God delivered me from the power of darkness into the kingdom of His dear Son, Jesus Christ of Nazareth, who is above all Col. 1:13.

Many false prophets shall rise like Prophet Guru, Prophet Confucius, and so on. Thank God, Christ is better than all prophets, for he created them all. Heb. 1:1-3, John 1:1-3.

Iniquity shall abound, no one needs a mirror to see the gravity of sins to sins, transgressions to transgressions, and iniquity to iniquity, which is now accepted as normal civilisation. Gays and homosexuals are the fashion of the present day, though vigorously condemned by God Rom 1:26-28 says "For this homosexual and lesbian acts, God gave them up, not looking at what they were doing, but reserving them for eternal condemnation unto vile affections; for even their women did change the natural use into that which is against nature;

"And likewise, also the man leaving the natural use of the woman, burned in their lust toward one another, men with men working that which is unseemly, and receiving in themselves that recompense of their error which was meet".

"And as they did not like to retain God in their knowledge, God also gave them over to a reprobate mind, to do those things which are not convenient". God gave them up to uncleanness through the lusts of their own hearts, to dishonour their own bodies between themselves, for they have changed the truth of God into a lie", they worshipped and served the creature rather than the Creator, who is blessed for ever" Rom. 1:24-28.

You are being warned. Take heed, lest any man deceive you. For many shall come in my name with signs, wonders, and miracles that without the discernment of the Spirit, you will accede that they are Christ's.

How do you know them, the Lord himself said that they will say it with their mouths that they are Christ's Mk. 13:6. Don't therefore doubt those children of God, given the power by the Lord as he said "He that believeth, and is baptised, shall be saved, but he that believeth shall be damned".

And these signs shall follow them that believe. In my name, shall they cast out devils; they shall speak with new tongues. Mk. 16:16-17.

WE ARE NOW IN PERILOUS TIMES

Men are lovers of themselves, men nowadays get a license to marry each other. Covetous, blasphemers, disobedient to parents, unthankful, unholy, despisers of those that are good, lovers of pleasure more than lovers of God, men of corrupt minds, reprobate concerning the faith. The Word of God says that "folly shall be manifest unto all men, as theirs also was 2 Tim. 3:1-5.

I ask you a question, which of the above are not true, yet they are words of your Creator mentioned over 2000 years ago, if you look at it. He that cometh from above is above all. He that is of the earth is earthly, and speaks of the earth; he that cometh from heaven is above all John 3;31. And Jesus Christ said "I am from above" John 8:23.

For his words, which is the Word of God, is quick and powerful, and sharper than any two-edged sword; piercing even to the dividing asunder of soul and spirit, and of the joints and marrow, and is a discerner of the thoughts and intents of the heart Heb. 4:12.

The Bible is the true Word of God, for when Christ was on the Calvary cross, there were over 20 prophecies of the Bible fulfilled to show who truly is the Son of the Mighty God.

Psalm 22:1 "My God my God, why hast thou forsaken me? Why art thou so far from helping me, and from the words of my roaring"? Mt. 27: 46 "E-li, E-li-la-ma sabachtani? My God, My God, why hast thou forsaken me?

Psalm 22:8 "He trusted in God; that he would deliver him; let him deliver him, seeing he delighted in him". Mt. 27:43 "He trusted in God, let him deliver him now, if he will have him; for he said I am the Son of God".

Isaiah 50:6 "I gave my back to the smiters, and my cheeks to them that plucked off the hair; I hid not my face from shame and spitting. Mt. 26:67 "Then they did spit in his face, and buffeted him; and others smote him with the palms of their hands".

Isaiah 53:9 "And he made his grave with the wicked, and with the rich in his death; because he had done no violence, neither was any deceit in his mouth. Mt. 27: 59-60 "And when Joseph of Arimathea had taken the body, he wrapped it in a clean linen cloth, and laid it in his own new tomb which he had hewn out in the rock, and he rolled a great stone to the door of the sepulchre and departed.

Isaiah 53:3. He is despised, and rejected of men; a man of sorrows, and acquainted with grief, and we hid as it were our faces from him; he was despised, and we esteemed him not. John 1:11. "He came unto his own, and his own received him not".

Zechariah 12:10 "And I will pour upon the house of David, and upon the inhabitants of Jerusalem, the spirit of Grace, and of supplications; and they shall look upon me whom they have pierced, and they shall mourn for him as one mourneth for his only son; and shall be in bitterness for him, as one that is in bitterness for his first born.

John 19:33-34. "But when they came to Jesus, and saw that he was dead already, they brake not his legs, but one of the soldiers with a spear pierced his side, and forthwith there came out blood and water.

WHAT BUSINESS HAS HE IN COMING

As the young men would say, he is not coming to rave. He had no part in raving, the King of Glory is coming on serious business to manifest himself to all eyes, while the hurly-burly is going on, while people are dining and wining, just as in the day of Noah. "He will come not as a babe born in Bethlehem, but as the Saviour, Lord and Judge".

He will no more be a fairy tale. He will be a reality. I will be able to say "I told them so".

He will not be a central figure in a beautiful story about Israel. He will be the one many will be hiding their faces from, while others are shouting Hallelujah to the Saviour. Those who beat me up because of Jesus will suck their fingers that day unless they change to Jesus.

Behold, he said, I come quickly, hold fast that which thou hast, that no man take thy crown. Believe you me, he is coming with various types of crowns for whatsoever one sows he will reap.

Whoever is honest, and does his work faithfully will receive a crown of honour, like Mordecai who went out from the presence of the King in royal apparel of blue and white, and with a great crown of gold, and with a garment of fine linen and purple Est. 8;15.

When the Chief Shepherd shall appear, he will come with the Crown of Glory 1 Peter 5:4.

To any one who did God's work conscientiously, the Crown of Righteousness is awaiting that person that day 2 Tim. 4:8.

Blessed is the man that endures temptations, for when he is tried, he shall receive the Crown of Life. Rev. 2:10.

For what is our hope, or joy, or crown of rejoicing? Are not even we in the presence of our Lord Jesus Christ at his coming 1 Thes. 2:19. There is happiness awaiting his believers, are you one?

All the above are what we should struggle to receive from him, but he is coming with crowns for children of disobedience, those who limit what God can have, and what he can't have; those who perish for lack of vision Prov. 29:18. He will give them the Crown of Demons Rev. 9:7. He will give them the Crown of Satan

Rev. 12:3. He will give them the Crown of Blasphemy Rev. 13:1.

He will give them the crown of thorns placed on Jesus Christ at the Calvary cross will be reversed on their heads Mt. 27:29.

They will receive the Crown of Corruption 1 Cor. 9:25.

Everybody knew that Jesus was the Lamb of God John 1:29, that was crucified for the first time on that cruel tree. He will not accede to such again a second time.

He is coming as the Lion of Judah Rev. 5;5. Even men do fear the Lion in the forest, but the Lion of Judah can no more be shut by the hunters. Being hunted and killed the first time, he reverses the position.

The first time he came as a servant, he said "For ever, the Son of man came not to be ministered unto, but to minister and to give his life a ransom for many" Mark 10:45.

The second time is different. He is coming to reign with might and power. "And the seventh angel sounded; and there were great voices in heaven; saying the kingdoms of this world are become the Kingdoms of our Lord, and of his Christ; and he shall reign for ever and ever Rev. 11:15.

The first time, as the Rock of Salvation "And I give unto them eternal life, and they shall never perish, neither shall any man pluck them out of my hand John 10:28.

The second time, as the Great Mountain that filled the whole earth Daniel 2:35.

First as meek and lowly Mt. 11:29 and Phil. 2:8. And being found in fashion as a man, he humbled himself, and became obedient unto death, even the death of the cross.

The second time to tread the winepress of vengeance of the Lord God Almighty Rev. 14;19 says "And the winepress was trodden without the city, and blood came out of the winepress, even unto the horse bridles, by the space of a thousand and six hundred furlongs. He will send his enemies to the lake of fire Rev. 19:20.

First time to be judged by wicked men. Then Pilate therefore took Jesus and scourged him, and the soldiers plaited a crown of thorns and put it on his head, and they put him on a purple robe John 19:1-2.

The second time to be the Judge of all men that ever walked on earth. Moses, Samuel, Elisha, John the Baptist, and other prophets and the other small gods John 5: 26-34.

First to die for our sins. The Bible says "For I delivered unto you first of all that which I also received, how that Christ died for our sins according to the Scriptures 1 Cor. 15:3.

The second time to be King of Kings, and Lords of Lords, the blessed and only Potentate 1 Tim. 6:15.

The first time, he was gone like the shadow when it was declineth; he was tossed up and down as the locust Ps. 109:23.

The second time to "Sit on his throne with him that overcometh as he overcome" Rev. 3:21.

He gives us great advice as he said that "He that hath an ear, let him hear what the Spirit saith unto the churches". Be prepared for His second coming, while the precious blood is still flowing with salvation and mercy that will lead you to eternal life. The battle between Christ and Satan had been won by the Son of God. You and I have a choice, thank God. I choose Christ as my Lord and Saviour.

I wish above all things, that those who have not yet done so, do likewise.

SEND THE LIGHT INTO MY LIFE

Who would not rejoice with a man born blind if someone came and opened his eyes? Most people would, but not everyone did when Christ Jesus who is above all did this to a man.

The man was happily praising God for what happened to him. People who knew him marvelled, asking themselves "Is not this that he was blind and begged"? Some were doubtful, others said it was not him whilst others said it was.

The healed man sang.

I am the blind man
Born absolutely blind
But now praising the Lord
For I can see you all

Jesus is the Healer
Who healed my blindness
I am really happy today
For I can see you all

The Jews were furious, "what shall we do to this Jesus?" He is now winning the whole populace; he needs to be eliminated from the earth, the quicker the better. Their excuse for not praising God for this miracle was that "it was on the Sabbath Day". The man who had just received sight answered them "I have lost the counting of days, for all other days were like Sabbath, for I could not see with my eyes what was going on, days in darkness look the same".

The Jews revealed how meagre their spiritual knowledge was , when they said that "they are Moses disciples forgetting or not knowing that Jesus said that the Lord spoke to him". "I will raise them up a Prophet from among their brethren, like unto thee, and I will put my words in his mouth; and he shall speak unto them all that I shall command him".

"And it shall come to pass, that whosoever will not hearken unto my words which I shall speak in my name, I will require it of him" Deut. 18:18-19. Just as they did not hearken.

The Pharisees asked him how he had received his sight, which he told them. "He put clay on mine eyes, and I washed and I see, it is as simple as that, with the hand of God".

It was too much for the Pharisees to be true, some of them burst out "This man is not of God; but thought they are" because Jesus keepeth not the Sabbath he instituted and abrogated. Then people began to see the driving force behind them, which is the spirit of jealousy by asking "How can a man that is a sinner do such miracles?" And, praise God, there was a division among them.

Those who believed were jumping for joy singing it loud and clear.

In the name of Jesus, send the light
Send the light
Send the Light
Into my life

The Pharisees were sweating, "What sayest thou of him; that he hath opened thine eyes?" He said that is incomparable to any one I know, He is a Prophet.

What? A Prophet? Yes, He is more than a Prophet, that is not without honour, but in his own country, and among his own kin, just as you Pharisees dishonour him, and also in his own house Mark 6:4. Once more, I say He is a Prophet.

The Jews still did not believe the man's testimony, they needed to call his parents even though many people had said he was, they failed to acknowledge the reality of the miracle of God.

We don't believe this is your son who ye say was born blind. How then doth he now see? Tell us for we have not seen anything like this before.

The parents answered "We know that this is our son, we cannot disown him. Believe it or not, he was born blind". "But one thing that baffles us as you is by what means he can now see, because we were not there when his healing took place". "Why not ask him yourselves as you can see he is now of age"

The parents were happy, but because they feared man more than God, they were unable to confess that Jesus Christ was the Great Physician that did it.

If you think that the devil is happy at your success, you must be joking. They called the man that had been healed, and told him to do what they failed to do. "Give God the praise". They said that they knew that Christ is a sinner, and they are holier than anyone else, even their maker and their God John 9:24.

The man's answer was sharp and concise. "Whether he be a sinner or not, I know not, but my concern is that whereas I was blind, now I see". "You are opposed to this miracle because He could do it but you cannot".

They said "Okay, we hear you, now tell us what did he to thee? How opened he thine eyes?" They at least recognised that he was the one born blind that could now see.

"I have told you many times, and ye pretended not to hear. Wherefore would ye hear it again? By the way, I have a question to ask you; Will you also be his disciples"? A bombshell to their hearing. They swore "never, never" and denounced him "Thou art his disciple", but we are Moses disciples", of which the Bible says "Christ was counted worthy of more glory than Moses, inasmuch as he who hath builded the house hath more honour than the house. Christ created Moses Heb. 3:3. John 1:3. Christ, in answer, said "Do not think that I will accuse you to the Father; there is one that accuseth you, even Moses in whom ye trust (John 5:45), who would say that he warned you about Jesus Dt. 18:18-19 to obey and follow him.

The man told them "In my eyes was darkness, now the light has shone on me; a marvellous thing, that ye know not from whence he is, for people perish for lack of knowledge" Hos. 4:6.

The Jews and Pharisees had no creditable replies to the man's answers, as he went on to say that God never bothered himself to listen to sinners' prayers, nor use him to do marvels as you see, but if a man be a worshipper of God, and doeth his will him he heareth.

Know for sure that, since the world began, it has never been told that any man opened the eyes of one that was born blind like himself. And I perceive that it is out of jealousy that you are saying these things. You know certainly that "If this man were not of God, he could do nothing, for the eyes of the Lord can not look on iniquity" Hab. 1:13.

Now ignorance of the scriptural knowledge revealed "Thou, including Jesus, wast altogether born in sins, and dost thou teach us? They lack the knowledge that they were shapen in iniquity, and in sin did their mother conceive them Ps. 51:5. Their holier than thou attitude was a sin on their part. They did not repent, they cast the man out. The Lord Jesus Christ saw him later and asked him "Dost thou believe on the Son of God"? And he answered and said "Who is he Lord"? Even in the spirit, he called Jesus "Lord" (before knowing who is) 1 Cor 12:3, that I might believe on him.

And Jesus said unto him "Thou hast both seen him, and it is he that is talking with thee". The man born blind, who Christ sent the light into his life said "Lord, I believe", and he worshipped him. Today, be not afraid. He can send his light into your life. He can send the light into your health, work, your troubled life, your home, and your ministry. Amen.

ONLY ONE WAY TO HEAVEN

Heaven is like an island, to which there is only a bridge leading to it. Anyone coming in to heaven must pass through the bridge. Don't think of an aeroplane, because there is no airport or heliport there.

One must pass through that bridge. The bridge to that beautiful city is equally very narrow, and only one vehicle plies the place.

No one can say that he cannot afford the fares, for you don't pay any fares to go there. The Pound Sterling, US dollar, Russian Rouble or French Franc cannot be exchanged there for they are worthless over there.

The transport there is free, and so also is the certainty of getting there, for there can be no accident or hindrance on the way to the city laid with gold purer than the one people struggle to have on earth. There, gold represents the sands on which we tread here on earth.

By the look of it, you can view how pleasant it will look. There is no sorrow there, death has been abrogated in the city.

Only one bridge leads to the Golden City, just as Jesus Christ is the only way to the Father. The city cannot be reached through any man, but through God who became man, being the Word of God that put on flesh. The word which was in the beginning John 1:1-14.

This Word of God boldly said that "He is the way, the truth and the life", and went further to say that he is the only bridge to that city where his Father dwells. "There is no other way to reach there but by him alone" John 14:6.

I read that statement and thought deeply about it. "I am the way", God says. No one else has said "They are the way", or there would be more than one way. On the earth here, many simply jump into different ways and find themselves at a cul-de-sac, or point of no return without reaching their destination; only to find themselves in the land of desolation, rather than the place full of milk and honey, i.e. in hell rather than in heaven.

Let us look at what Religious Leaders said about the way. They all knew how important the way is.

Confucius said "he knows the way". He confessed that he is not the way, but he knows the way, and whoever of his followers that wants to go on the right way should go to Jesus who proved himself by his death, burial and resurrection, that he is above all impediments waiting to take you to the City of God.

Krishna said he can show his followers the way. They may consider him a way to reach The Way, who is the Son of God, who said it boldly that "Unless they come to him as the Truth, they would not have eternal life for He is the Way, the Truth, and the Life" John 14:6. Krishna points to the way, he says "Go to Jesus who is the way".

Rev. Moon said "He sees the Way". Seeing is not the same as being on the way, unless they quickly jump to the way, accepting Christ as their Lord and Saviour. He and his followers will find themselves eliminated from the Kingdom of God, anyone can see Westminster Palace, but not everyone can enter into the palace and sleep there for a day.

Mohammed said "He is the Prophet of the way", and in Surat Fahat said "God, show us the way". There is no point asking God to show him the way, when God said of Jesus "This is my beloved son, in whom I am well pleased, ye hear him" Mt. 17:5. And the Quran says that Jesus Christ, the Way, is a sign for all peoples, Jews and Gentiles alike (Surat 21), Anbiyaa Verse 91, so everybody must follow him.

The Way commanded everyone to follow him. God will love all who follow Jesus, and forgive their sins, for God is a forgiver, and the most merciful (Surat 3) Al-Imran Vs. 31.

The Quran went further to say that "And there is none of the people of the Book, i.e. all the prophets; But must believe in Jesus before they die. For, on the day of judgement, Christ will be a witness against them Q4, Nisda Verse 159.

If he said that his Father (God) "judgeth no man, but hath committed all judgement unto the Son" John 5:22, then you must seek Jesus' face to get to heaven.

The truthful witness can in court free someone or send them to prison. Christ is your Judge, whether you mind it or not.

The Quran is quite explicit when it said "And Jesus shall be a sign for the coming of the hour of Judgement". Therefore, have no doubt about the hour, but follow ye him, for this is a straight way. Surat 43 Zukhruf Vs. 61.

If the Quran says that "He, Jesus, is the straight way, why do people deviate from The Way, and look for the way they already know. Christ Jesus is The Way, who commanded everyone to stop disputing. Fear God, and obey him Surat 43 vs. 61 & 63.

And God himself, speaking said to Jesus "Christ, O Jesus, I will take thee, and raise thee to myself, and clear thee of the falsehoods of those who blaspheme. I will make those who follow thee superior to those who reject faith. To the day of resurrection; then shall ye all return unto me; And I will judge between you of the matters wherein ye dispute. Surat 3 Alimran Vs. 55.

The simple fact is that he is described as, not only the Way, but the Quran says that he is "the straight way" Surat 4:61. If God says that He is the Straight Way, then all others are crooked ways.

Buddha said that "He is seeking the way". He did not say he is the way. The way is not far from anyone who wants to go to the way. Christ Jesus said "I am the Way, the Truth, and the Life. Come unto me all ye that labour and are heavy laden, and I will give you rest",

Take my yoke upon you, and learn of me, for I am meek and lowly in heart; and ye shall find rest unto your souls.

For my yoke is easy, and my burden is light Matt. 11:28-30. The Bible says that the Lord is with you, while ye be with him, and if ye seek him, he will be found of you 2 Chro. 15:2(b).

New Age Movement said "Come, let us travel together on the way". They cannot say that the way for the way is quite different from a way. Many find a way, without finding The Way, and quite rightly as the Quran said, Christ is the Straight Way.

One should be saddened about how man looks for comfort, and not the salvation which brings perfect and permanent comfort. I saw on the television how Indus in India made Jesus Christ a subject of devotion. They said that 80% of them believe that Baby Jesus answers prayers, that he never abandons them, that they never went away disappointed, and that the Hindus are coming from America, Australia, and Canada. I wouldn't be surprised if those from London go as well. The fact is that At the name of Jesus Christ, every knee should bow, of things in heaven, and things in earth, and things under the earth. And that every tongue should confess that Jesus Christ is Lord to the glory of God the Father Phil. 2:10-11.

The fact is that not everyone that says LORD, Lord, shall inherit the Kingdom of God, but those who do the will of the Father in heaven Matt 7:21.

They said that the Catholics there on exchange, also acquired Hindu customs, distributing flowers etc. it is said, that "when in Rome, do as the Romans do" but would it be wise to go to a land where, say, murder is the norm, and join in committing murders?

The Hindus in India need to know who Jesus Christ is. He is no longer a baby. He is now the Wonderful Counsellor that moves all our sorrow; the Mighty God whose power is beyond all idols that have eyes, but cannot see, ears but cannot speak. Jer. 10:1-9. Let them know that Jesus Christ is the same yesterday, today and forever Heb. 13:8.

Let them know that he is, that lives, and was dead; and they should behold him for he is alive forever more. Let them realise that he holds the key of hell and of death Rev. 1:18.

Let them know that he is the resurrection and the life, that if they believe in him that He is the Son of God, although they were dead, yet shall they live John 11:25. Let them know that it is time to abandon idols which profiteth not.

Let them know that He is the Prince of Peace, who guides our feet in the way of peace, the Author of Peace 1 Cor. 14:33.

Let them know that they cannot have peace, apart from the Owner of peace who left peace with us, who gives his peace to us, not as the world (deceivers) giveth, give he unto us; When we believe him, we should not let our hearts be troubled, neither let it be afraid John 14:27, then our peace and joy shall be full John 16:24.

Finally, let them know that they should not be afraid of their idols, for they cannot do evil; neither is it in them to do good Jer. 10:5(b).

Don't be misled by human doctrines of the Christian Science, nor what the Unity says. Spiritualism is obviously demonic. Theosophy is saying what they don't inwardly believe that, in time, they will become Christ. Will go to the Calvary cross as well? The answer to that is "no", for there is only one Saviour, Jesus Christ Acts 4:12.

The Rosicrucians comparing Christ with the sun failed to realise that Jesus Christ made the sun, and not only the Begotten Son of God, but we should ask them if they mention any other conceived of the Holy Ghost of God. God had only one begotten Son, but the devil has many.

Bahalism. They believe in many Messiahs, so we have heard of many different Jesus of various places. They all died, and their bones are in their wicked graves. Liars they all turned out to be. They misled people, and surely the Lord Jesus will judge them. They will know who is Lord.

The leader of Bahal died and is now in an abyss, awaiting the judgement of Jesus Christ. John 5:20-22.

Mormonism said Jesus is both the Father, and the Son. "liars". Who was Jesus referring to when he mentioned "My Father", or when he was teaching the Lord's prayer, or when he said "You must do the will of the Father", while he was down here on earth. They seem not to know that they, as individuals, are body, soul and spirit - three different things. God the Father is different from God the Son, and God the Holy Spirit.

Unilaterism said that their birth is just as divine as that of Jesus, yet each and everyone of them had their own earthly father. They seemed not to know the meaning of 'divine', i.e. 'god-like'. On this, I ask them how about all our human imperfections i.e. lying, anger, bitterness? Does this make us divine. No human being is divine, but rather we are all natural and act in the flesh often. Claiming divinity is a sin against the Holy Spirit, and God will judge them. John 5:22, Mt. 12:31-32.

Modernism says that Christ is so good, and not bad as humans are; that God's goodness deludes us to take him as a god. No one took him as God without the power or ability to walk or touch, but as the Mighty God Isa. 9:6. He is God, even before he came to the World. Like it or not, he is what he is, "The Almighty God and the Prince of Peace". These titles weren't carved out by Christians.

No man can be good. Modernism just brings self-destruction, sexual perversion, and love of the world which again leads to destruction. Modernism without Christ is total destruction. Mt. 12:31-32.

Christadelphianism also said that Christ is not divine. How do they know? Is it by eyes which cannot see, or by their carnal mind which is enmity against God? Rom. 8:7. They are sinning against the Holy Spirit, and it is unpardonable.

Seventh Day Adventist claim that, in Jesus humanity, he partook of sinful fallen nalure.

The Bible says that "For we have not an high priest which cannot be touched with the feeling of our infirmities; but was in all points tempted like as we are, YET WITHOUT SIN Heb. 4:15

Christ himself asked them a question "Which of you convicteth him of sin? And if he says the truth, why do ye not believe him?" John 8:46. Christ is sinless, pure and holy.

What the above amounts to is the fact that "The thief comes not but to steal, to kill and to destroy; but thank God, that Christ came that those who believe him that is sinless, may have life and have it more abundantly" John 10:10. It is the devil that makes humans categorise Jesus Christ, as the devil himself and his children.

I would refer you to Christ's words "Wherefore I say unto you, "All manner of sin and blasphemy shall be forgiven unto men; but the blasphemy against the Holy Spirit shall not be forgiven unto men".

"And whosoever speak a word against the Son of man, it shall be forgiven him; but whosoever speaketh against the Holy Ghost, it shall not be forgiven him, neither in this world, neither in the world to come" Mt. 12:31-32.

It is time to change to Christ Jesus from the dilemma of Satanic doctrines. Christ is waiting for you, and that is today. You need to hear the Word of God in a place where the Word is taught in spirit and in truth. Don't allow Satan to tie you down as a ram ready for slaughter.

Remember to enter at the straight gate; for wide is the gate and broad is the gate that leads to destruction, and many there be which will go in thereat.

Because straight is the gate, and narrow is the way which leads unto life, and few there be that find it. Matt. 7:14-15.

I sincerely invite you to join me at the narrow way of Jesus where there is life; for in Him is life, where there is peace; for He is the Prince of Peace Isa. 9:6. Where there is healing; for he is the Great Physician 1 Pet. 2:24.

The way through the narrow gate has room for you, and I say to those who are yet to enjoy the value of Jesus, come and meet the Wonderful Jesus Christ of Nazareth, Son of the Mighty God who is above all things.

THIS NEWS MUST BE HIDDEN

It is normal for everyone to rejoice at good news, but this particular news turned to sorrow for his enemies.

The first day of the week came Mary Magdalene, and the other Mary to see the Sepulchre.

And behold, there was a great earthquake; for the angel of the Lord descended from heaven. His countenance was like lightning, and his raiment as white as snow.

It was not a usual thing to see angels, so the messengers of the chief priests who were sat on watch, were paralysed with fear. Having seen what had happened, they believed that "Surely, this is the Son of God" Amen.

The angel reassured the women "Fear not, for I know that ye seek Jesus, which was crucified".

They said "Why seek ye the living among the dead? He is not here but is risen; remember how he spake unto you when he was yet in Galilee, saying the Son of Man must be delivered into the hands of sinful men, and be crucified, and the third day rise again". Mk. 16:5-6.

The women then returned from the sepulchre, and told the disciples of the Good News, however, like many doubters about resurrection today; they too took it as idle tales. They had only heard of Lazarus being raised by Christ before. The Bible says that they did not believe the ladies" Lk. 24:11, Mk. 16:11.

Then rose Peter and John, and ran into the sepulchre where they found the linen clothes lying, and they went away into their own home.

Mary came back weeping at the sepulchre. She stooped down and looked inside where she saw two angels in white, sitting at the head and foot of the tomb where the body of Jesus had lain.

The angels asked her the cause of her weeping, and she told them "They have taken away my Lord, and I know not where they have taken him". Turning back, she saw Jesus who said "Woman, why weepest thou, whom seekest thou". She thought Jesus was the gardener and she said "Sir, if thou hast borne him, tell me where thou hast laid him, and I will take him away".

Jesus called her "Mary", she turned herself, and saith unto him "Rab-bo-mi, i.e. "Master"! Jesus said to her "Touch me not, for I am not yet ascended to my Father, but go to my brethren, and say unto them, I ascend unto my Father and your Father, and to my God and your God" John 20:15-17.

TOUCH ME NOT

Meet me in Galilee. Between the time Mary went to tell the Good Tidings of Resurrection to the disciples, and her meeting Jesus Christ in Galilee, the Lord had gone to heaven to report to the Father.

In the twinkling of an eye, he was back 1 Cor 15:52(a).

He went and told the Father "The work of salvation is completed. Now the devil is put to open shame" Col. 2:15. "Having spoiled principalities and powers, I made a show of them openly, triumphing over them in it. Father, the world has seen the limitation of Satan's power. Now, I have to go and meet my disciples, you have chosen for me. Within the minute, he was back on earth straight to Galilee.

Remember, that your prayer through the name of the Lord Jesus is carried to heaven within a second.

THIS NEWS MUST NOT BE KNOWN

"Surely, the Lord bringeth the counsel of the heathen to nought; he maketh the devices of the people of none effect, the counsel of the Lord standeth for ever" Psalm 33:10-11.

It is therefore obvious that God hath raised up Jesus, having loosed the pains of death because it was not possible that he should be holden of it, his soul could not be left in hell.

The Elders of Israel did not want to have anything to do with the resurrection. They tried to keep the body of Jesus in the tomb, but they had no power to withhold him whom God hath raised up. They stooped as low as to bribe the soldiers who came to give the news they did not like to hear.

They hoped it was not true that Jesus Christ of Nazareth had resurrected. The soldiers gave an account of the earthquake, and how the graves were opened. About how Jesus Christ was even in the grave "the Lord who preached unto the dead, that they might be judged by him according to men in the flesh; but live in the grave according to God in the spirit until resurrection day"1 Peter 4:6.

On hearing the news, the elders must have been wetting themselves. They were sore fearful that they would lose all their authority and possibly be stoned if the populace heard that Christ had arisen.

The device was "Do not tell anyone about the resurrection of Jesus", just tell people that his disciples came to steal his body from the tomb while you were asleep.

The soldiers objected, and said they would rather speak the truth as the possibility of all of them sleeping at the same time was remote. They also were fearful of the Governor learning that they were asleep when they were supposed to be guarding Jesus body.

The elders assured them that they would persuade the Governor not to punish them, and that they would be rewarded if they lied. So the soldiers took the money, and did as they were told.

Jesus said "For there is nothing hidden, which shall not be made manifest, neither is there anything kept secret, but that it should come abroad" Mk. 4:22.

The chief priest's deceit is commonly reported among the Jews until this day Mt. 28:11-15.

HOW THE RESURRECTION OF JESUS WAS KNOWN BY THE POPULACE

To every action, there is an equal and opposite reaction. The giving of the money to the soldiers produced a great reaction. It made the people know that Jesus Christ resurrected, rather than keep it secret.

The soldiers did go home with large sums of money Mt. 28:12, but their families wanted to know where they got the money from. Their wives pestered them until one of them shared the secret with his wife, i.e. "The whole nation shed innocent blood by crucifying Jesus Christ of Nazareth whom I can now confirm is truly the Son of God".

"For the past three days we have been guarding his grave. As we were talking, there was a great earthquake as the angel of the Lord descended from heaven and came and rolled back the stone upon which he then sat". The soldier must have said to his wife "I tell you the truth, Jesus is arisen indeed"! Mt. 28:11-15.

The Bible says that "The love of money is the root of all evil which, while some coveted after, they have erred from the faith and pierced themselves through with many sorrows 1 Tim. 6:10. The soldiers and their wives were suddenly living luxuriously like lottery winners, and the people were murmuring about the source of their sudden riches.

Eventually, the news was spread from wives, to parents, to broader family, until the whole nation heard the news.

However, the soldiers were not the only witnesses. Mary Magdalene saw the resurrected Jesus Christ, who assured her "All hail, be not afraid; go tell my brethren that they go into Galilee, and there they shall see me" Mt. 28: 9-10.

Mary Magdalene and the other Mary also saw Jesus as they were going home to the disciples to give the good news Mt. 27:51.

Jesus also appeared to two disciples going to Emmaus Mk. 16:12-13

Jesus appeared to Peter Lk. 24:34.

He appeared to ten apostles in the Upper Room Lk. 24:36. "Peace be unto you, and receive ye the Holy Ghost".

To the eleven apostles in the Upper Room Mk. 16:14.

To Thomas Jn. 20:26-27

To seven apostles at the Sea of Tiberias Jn. 21:1-24.

To eleven apostles on a mountain in Galilee Mt. 28:16-20.

To five hundred brethren at once 1 Cor. 15:6.

To Paul 1 Cor.15:8.

To all that were present on His ascension. Acts 1:9-11.

Last but not the least, to the resurrected saints who came to the Holy City and appeared unto many. When people saw Elisha, Elijah, Moses, Jeremiah, King David, Abraham, Isaac and Jacob, and many that believed unto Jesus as He preached to them, visiting their relatives; also preaching that the grave received the greatest visitor that would every pay it a visit when Jesus Christ came there; and that they believed him that He is the Saviour, the King of Kings and the Lord of lords, the Glorious Son of God who is above death and the grave.

Telling their families "You have the opportunity while you are alive, that He will not be visiting the graves no more for the grave could not hold Him. They were telling people that "We are in the last day of grace". For "To this end, Christ both died, and rose, and revived that he might be Lord, both of the dead and living Rom. 14:9. Hence, he became qualified to judge any man that ever stepped on earth.

He was seen of Saul of Tarsus, who became Paul the apostle of Jesus. Whether the devil likes it or not, Christ resurrected and the good news is known all over the world today; the unbelievers know, but the news is too great for them to fathom since their leaders bones are still in the grave awaiting the day of resurrection and judgement of Christ.

Today, this message of death and his resurrection is to them that perish, foolishness; but unto us that are saved, it is the power of God which destroys the wisdom of the wise, and brings to nothing the understanding of the prudent. 1 Cor. 1:18-19.

The Pharisees and Jesus knew that Christ died, was buried and resurrected. You too must believe and reap the benefit, which is the salvation of your soul.

THESE SIGNS SHALL FOLLOW THEM

Jesus Christ, giving his last order to the disciples that they should go and do all that they have seen him do, and say all that they have heard him say.

He did not let them go without an assurance that he would not leave them powerless. He knew that without the Instrument of Office, which is the Holy Spirit, they would all simply disperse and go into oblivion.

He therefore told them that "Signs and wonders shall follow them, that people would know that He was the Sender". He said that "In his name would they cast out demons, in his name those under the bondage of the devils would be released".

For them to know that he is not a man that he should lie, and neither is he the Son of Man that he should repent that which he hath said; and shall he not do it? Or hath he spoken and shall he not make it good? Numbers 23:19. The first sign would be their speaking in new tongues. One wonders what Thomas would have been thinking about this tongue business before he spoke it!

Sign two was that they would take up serpents, and if they drank any deadly thing it would not hurt them.

The last sign was that they would lay hands on the sick, and they would recover. Mk. 16:17-18.

His words stand for ever and ever. The disciples obeyed his commandment "Stay in Jerusalem".

And when the promise was to be fulfilled, the disciples were in the upper room, and suddenly there came a sound from heaven as of a mighty rushing wind; and it filled all the house where they were sitting.

And they saw cloven tongues like as of a fire, and it sat upon each of them, and they were all filled with the Holy Ghost, and began to speak with other tongues as the Spirit gave them utterance; thus the first sign mentioned by Jesus Christ came to reality. This must have given them confidence that the other signs would come to pass.

It was a perfect day when Jews, devout men out of every nation under heaven were present in Jerusalem, for it was the day of Pentecost.

Every man heard them speak in his own language, amazed that the people were in no way related to them, and had no cause to speak in languages which they had never learnt.

Many were happy and wanted to know what was going on, whilst others mocked them saying they were drunkards full of new wine. This still happens today.

Peter, now full of the Holy Ghost lifted up his voice, addressed them on what had happened. How Jesus they crucified had sent what the people had witnessed to them in fulfilment of his promise Joel 2:28-29.

Full of confidence he said "Christ has arisen, having loosed the pains of death because it was not possible that he should be holden of it".

Peter told them God's promise concerning Jesus, as prophesied by David, that Christ would die, be buried, and He would be raised up to sit on God's throne. That his soul was not left in hell, neither did his flesh see corruption.

He emphasised that Jesus Christ is Lord, as the Lord God said to the Lord Jesus, "Sit thou on my right hand, until I make thy enemies thy footstool" Acts 2:34-35.

That all the house of Israel should know assuredly that God hath made Jesus whom they crucified, both Lord and Christ Acts 2:36.

He told them to repent and be baptised, every one of them "In the Name of Jesus Christ" for the remission of sins, and they would receive what they then received, which is the Holy Ghost.

Immediately, those who gladly received the Word were baptised, and about three thousand souls were added to the Church.

The second sign to manifest did not take many days. There was a lame man from his birth, a beggar at the Beautiful Gate, well known by all going in to pray at the temple.

We must realise that the Jews, the Pharisees, the Chief Priests were all inside the temple before Peter and John. They would be there earlier than others to light candles, incense; and do whatever else they needed to do before others came in.

Peter and John were delayed when the lame man asked for alms from them. Peter had not planned to heal or perform any miracle when they left home; but the anointing of the Holy Ghost rose in him, and he said to the lame man as he looked upon him with John, you too should look on us. How happy would the lame man have been to hear "Look on us". To him it must have meant at least a piece of silver since others would simply drop a few pence on his alms cloth.

He gave heed unto them, expecting something that is substantial. He did obey, and obedience is better than sacrifice 1 Sam. 15:22.

He got what seemed a rude shock when Peter said "Silver and gold have I none". The lame man probably wondered why they were wasting his time then.

Peter, seeing his reaction spoke on "but, such as I have give I thee. In the name of Jesus Christ of Nazareth, Rise up and walk".

Peter, following the great Pentecostal speech knew that "Greater is he that is in him, than he that is in the world" 1 John 4:4. He took the lame man by the right hand and lifted him up; and immediately, his feet and ankle bones received strength.

The lame man did not say "You see me lame, how can I rise up and walk"? He didn't ask to be left alone. Rather, the Bible says that he leapt up, stood, and then walked and entered with Peter and john INTO the temple; walking and leaping, and praising God.

He sang:-

I am delivered in his name
Once I was a lame man
I couldn't rise from the floor
Now I am delivered, Praise the Lord!

This man was jumping as though it was a dream, shouting beyond the voice of the rest of the congregation. People knew that something different took place; the name of Jesus Christ had manifested a great marvel beyond doubt.

Many were saying "I seem to know you, but the one who looked like you was lame". The man said "Yes, it was me, but Christ had raised me up through the hand of his disciples". This was another great opportunity to preach in the name dreaded by the Chief Priests, i.e. Jesus of Nazareth.

Someone said "You are a cheat, we never knew that you could walk, jump and run".

The man said "No, I have just been healed in the name of Jesus of Nazareth". The man became the talk of the town. Hallelujah.

The Lord Jesus said "All manner of blasphemy and sin shall be forgiven unto men; but the blasphemy against the Holy Ghost shall not be forgiven unto men Mt. 12:31-32.

There came the time when the disciples honesty came into test. They agreed to contribute into the coffers so that there could be meat in the house of God. Ananias and his wife Saphira sold their possessions. Instead of revealing the truth of how much they sold their possessions for, they chose to deceive the hosts of God.

Ananias came in, having kept part of the sale price, and gave up what he and his wife had agreed upon. Instead of being praised, he was nakedly exposed by the Holy Ghost, as Peter said "Ananias, why hath Satan filled thine heart to lie to the Holy Ghost, and to keep back part of the price of the land? Thou hast not lied unto men, but unto God."

And Ananias, hearing these words, fell down and gave up the ghost and died! And great fear fell on all them that heard these things.

His wife was at home, dressing up as a rich man's wife to come and receive the praises of men. When asked how much the land was sold for, she also in deceit lied like her husband had done. Peter said to her "How is it that ye have agreed together to tempt the Spirit of the Lord"? He said "Behold, the feet which have buried thy husband are at the door, and shall carry thee out".

"Then she fell down straight away at his feet, and yielded up the ghost, and the young men came in, and found her dead and took her and buried her by her husband".

This shows us that we should not serve the Lord with our mouth and lips only. Our hearts must be close to him, serving him in truth and in spirit Acts 5:1-11, Matt. 15:8.

Wonders of God can never cease, and He is no respecter of persons, time or place. Believers were the more added to the Lord insomuch that they brought forth the sick into the streets, and laid them on beds and couches that, at the least, the shadow of Peter passing by might overshadow some of them, bringing about their healing.

"Out of the cities, round about into Jerusalem, bringing sick folks, and them which were vexed with unclean spirits; and they were healed every one.

And there at Lydia, Peter found a certain man named Ae-neas, sick of palsy for eight years. Peter told him "Ae-neas, Jesus Christ maketh thee whole; arise and make thy bed". And the man arose immediately, and all Lyd-da and Sar-on saw Aeneas and turned unto the Lord.

At Joppa, a devout woman named Tabitha, full of good works was sick and died. She was laid in an upper chamber. They sent unto Peter to come very urgently. When Peter went he was immediately confronted with the corpse of Tabitha.

Was Peter afraid? No. He had seen his master, Jesus, who is above death, raise the son of the widow of Nain. He was there when Jesus called Lazarus from the grave.

Peter put all the people around forth, and kneeled down, and prayed; and turning him to the body said "Tabitha arise", and she opened her eyes; and when she saw Peter she sat up, and he gave her his hand and lifted her up. He called the saints and widows, then presented her alive Acts 9:36-43.

The Book of Exodus 14:14 said "The Lord shall fight for you, and ye shall hold your peace". All that was happening through the hands of the disciples obviously did not please the Authority who were loosing large members of their congregations; they thought they had got rid of Jesus, but the disciples were many doing the work of God.

Herod, the King, wanting a show, got hold of Peter to be sacrificed as usual on a feast day, putting him in prison after he had killed James the brother of John with the sword, to the joy of the Jews.

So that Peter wouldn't escape, he was guarded by sixteen soldiers in a secure prison. Although Herod thought the prison was as secure as safety itself, the prayer of the Saints was going on for Peter's safety. The angel of the Lord said unto him "Gird thyself and bind on they sandals, and cast thy garment about thee and follow me". To Peter it was like a vision.

He went out and followed the angel. After going past the first and second ward, they came unto the iron gate that lead into the city. The gates opened to them of its own accord ; "Open ye gates, and ye be lifted up to allow a child of God out of prison of man". They went out and the angel departed from Peter to go and show himself to the disciples.

Herod sought for Peter and found him not. He examined the keepers, and commanded that they should be put to death. The Lord said that "He will give men as a ransom for our lives". So he did in this case. His word is true for ever.

Jesus Christ gave us power to loose and bind. "Whatsoever ye shall bind on earth shall be bound in heaven; and whatsoever ye shall loose on earth shall be loosed in heaven Mt. 18:18.

Elymas, the sorceror withstood Paul, willing to turn Ser-gi-us Paulus from the faith. Paul, filled with the Holy Ghost, set his eyes on him and said "O ye full of subtlety and all mischief, thou child of the devil, thou enemy of all righteousness; will thou not cease to pervert the right ways of the Lord?

And now, behold, the hand of the Lord is upon her "And she shall be blind" not seeing the sun for a season. Immediately, there fell on him a mist and a darkness; and he went about seeking some to lead him by the hand. Thus Paul loosed the blind spirit on him Acts 13:11.

It came to pass that a damsel possessed with a spirit of divination met Paul and Silas at Macedonia. She followed them and cried, saying "These men are the servants of the most High God, which shew us unto the way of salvation" This sounded good, but her motive was to let people see her in the same light, serving the same God with Paul and Silas.

She really meant business, for she followed them many days saying that she shared the same spirit with Paul and Silas, so that her masters would have more gains.

Paul was grieved, and knew that "whatever we bind on earth would be bound in heaven" turned and said to the spirit "I command thee in the name of Jesus Christ to come out of her". And the spirit came out of her the same hour, she was tripped naked of the evil spirit. It is of a fact that the Lord's word can never fail. Acts 16:16-24.

Thus, the lady tried to match the Spirit of God with the spirit of divination and failed. Hallelujah.

In another episode, deceivers were exposed to the world to see. There were certain vagabonds, Jews, exorcists who took upon them, which had evil spirits, the name of the Lord. They thought that whatever Paul was doing, they could do it better; but the Lord knows those who serve him in truth and in spirit Matt. 15:8.

They, the seven sons of Sceva said to the evil spirits that "They adjure the spirits by Jesus whom Paul preacheth". Surely, the devils are not dummies, they know till today that it is the name of Jesus they bow to, not to anything else.

The evil spirit answered that he knew Jesus and Paul, but he didn't know these deceivers, then he leapt on them and overcame them. He prevailed against them so that they fled out of the house naked and wounded Acts 19:14-16.

The evil spirit exposed the seven sons of Sceva as belonging to him, having no connection with Jesus, they were not abiding in Jesus, neither he in them. They could not reap the rewards of deliverance of the Lord. Without Jesus, they could do nothing John 15:4-5.

Paul was faced with a position that could make people question the healing and deliverance power of the Lord. In the middle of a Gospel meeting, Eutycus slept and fell through the third floor window and was taken up dead.

Paul went down, and fell on him, and embraced him then said "Trouble not yourselves, for his life is in him". As he went up again, many would be wondering why he did not bring Eutycus if his life was in him.

He was never ruffled, he broke bread and ate, and had time to talk a long while, even till break of day when he departed.

The people went down and brought Eutycus alive. We saw our Lord Jesus Christ of Nazareth raised up the dead. Peter raised up the dead, we are assured that the same Spirit is in us, we too can do the works of the Lord with signs, wonders and miracles following us if we yield ourselves as tools worthy for use.

CHRIST ASCENDED INTO HEAVEN

There is no doubt in the believers' mind as to who will go to heaven to bring Christ Jesus to the earth, for everyone knows that He chose to come to bring salvation; and will come the second time again.

We equally know that there is no need to send anyone into the deep again, for Jesus spent three days in the deep preaching to the Spirits in captivity, and depriving the grave of its power of destruction. In this, he brought up the dead Saints in resurrection and they visited the Holy City.

It is written that "No man hath ascended up to heaven, but he Jesus that came down from heaven, even the Son of man which is in heaven; who made heaven and earth his home, who never lost contact with heaven". Who said that "He can do nothing of himself, but what he sees the Father do; for whatsoever he doeth, these also doeth the son likewise".

The Father loveth him, and sheweth him all things that he himself doeth. You can only be with someone to know what he is doing, and surely God, the Father is in heaven, and Jesus is with him.

He gathered the disciples together one day to let them know the advantages in his ascension, that unless he went away, the Holy Ghost will not come unto them; but if he departed, he would send the Holy Ghost to them. An event which took place on the Day of Pentecost. Acts 2.

He never hid the fact that he had to go back to where he came from, a place where he belonged. "I am not of this world, ye are from beneath, crated out of soil; I am from above". We know that after a visit to a place, you have to go back to where you came from; and heaven was where Jesus came from John 8:23.

John the Baptist said that Jesus Christ came from above, and he that came from above is above all; for he that is of the earth i.e. earthly, and speakest of the earth. He, Jesus, that came from heaven is above all John 3:31.

As the crucifixion was near, he explained the power and benefits in his ascension "Verily, verily I say unto you, he that believeth on me, the works I do; miracles that I do, healing that I heal, the blessings that I bless. My wish above all things, that thou mayest prosper and be in health even as thy soul prospereth" 3 John 2 Shall he that believeth on me do, because I ascend unto my father.

He stretched further a big advantage, "Whatsoever ye shall ask in my name, that will I do; that the Father may be glorified in the Son". Also, "if ye ask anything in my name, at which every knee shall bow, I will do it; know fully well that I shall be sitting on the throne of mercy in heaven above" Rev. 6:16 – and he is waiting for your requests.

Then forty days after the resurrection, the Lord who is above death, and above the clutch of the grave, was to go back to heaven.

He called his followers to tell them that they were not ignorant of the pending ascension; in that he had told them all things, and they have seen all things proved infallibly to them.

He therefore gave a command for them not to depart from Jerusalem "Whatever fear you may have, do remain in Jerusalem, for there the Promise of the Father, i.e. the Holy Ghost of which you have heard of will meet you". And Jesus truly baptised with the Holy Ghost not many days hence, i.e. the next ten days.

The disciples were not interested in the Holy Ghost, all they wanted was the restoration of the Kingdom of Israel. Christ told them that this was in his father's power to do. "Ye shall receive power after the Holy Ghost is come upon you; and ye shall be witnesses unto me, both in Jerusalem and in all Judaea, and in Samaria, and into the uttermost part of the earth Acts 1:8.

And when he had spoken these things, the transportation vehicle arrived, the people perhaps expecting a modern day rocket were surprised when the Cloud came down. They were gazing upwards steadfastly towards heaven. Their amazement came to an end when two angels in a white apparel said "Ye men of Galilee, why stand ye gazing up into heaven"? This same Jesus which is taken up from you into heaven, shall so come in like manner as ye have seen him go unto heaven Acts 1:11.

Everyone knows the battle between Christ and the devil. Just as you defeat him in one way, thus he will come again; that ye must be sober. Be vigilant because your adversary the devil, a roaring lion walketh about, seeking whom he may devour 1 Peter 5:8.

The devil waylaid the Lord, his maker, who spoilt his three-day party after the resurrection. Obviously, he does not possess all knowledge and, unknown to him, all power in heaven and earth had been given to Jesus Mt. 28:18.

He, like a beaten foe decided they shall both remain on earth because he was aware of the power of resurrection from the throne above. He, out of desperation went to the gates of heaven where the last battle took place, and the victory was won by the Lord who always wins.

A command from Jesus broke Satan's back "Lift up your heads O ye gates; and be ye lifted up ye everlasting doors; and the King of Glory shall come in".

Satan asked, although he knew already, "Who is the King of Glory"? Then Jesus answered "It is I the Lord, strong and mighty, the Lord mighty in battle". Remember the past feuds that you have lost Satan, "It is I the Lord, righteous whose right hand is become glorious in power, whose right hand hath dashed the enemy into pieces". Still the devil blocked the gate.

The Lord Jesus commanded again "Lift up your heads, O ye gates, even lift them up ye everlasting doors, and the King of Glory shall come in; and be exalted above the heavens, and his glory be above all the earth.

The devil asked again "Who is the King of Glory". Christ answered "I am the Lord of Hosts, Jesus Christ of Nazareth who conquered death, who resurrected from the grave; who is now going back to sit on my throne in heaven; I am the King of Glory". Satan then believed and he trembled and fled.

Then a cloud received him out of the disciples and followers sight, and thereby ascended on high, whereby he led captivity captive, stripped Satan of his power. Now we have freedom from Satan's oppression, we no more belong to the slave driver. We have received the gift of adoption; we are no more in bondage and no longer need to fear. The spirit of adoption gives us the boldness to cry Abba, Father, and receive answers to our petitions".

Glory be to Jesus Christ who is above any impediments of the devil, Hallelujah.

The Son of God is now sitting on the right hand of God, pleading our cause and awaiting our petitions Rom. 8:34.

CHRIST'S POWER IS UNLIMITED

Can you ever imagine going into the fire without being burned? Yes Jesus did so to rescue God's children. He did this in his capacity as Jehovah Emmanuel, which means "God is with us" Matt 1:23.

Nebuchadnez-zar, stirred by the spirit of pride, made an image of gold, and gathered together princes, governors, captains, judges, the treasurers, the counsellors, the sheriffs, and all the rulers of the provinces for the dedication of his idol. The handiwork of man which, having eyes see not, having ears, hear not, standing in one place, but cannot move, neither can it remember anything. Mk. 8:18.

There at the dedication, Nebuchadnez-zar made a law that at a certain time, when people hear the sound of the cornet, flute, harp, or psaltery, they should not be dancing; but fall down and worship the golden image that he had set up. This is the custom of the people, which are vain, that they cutteth a tree out of the forest, deck it with silver and gold, fasten it with nails and hammers that it moves not. Upright as the palm tree, but speaks not, they must be borne (carried) because they cannot go anywhere Jer. 10:3-4. They were just dummies yet the king commanded that whoever did not bow to their image should be cast into the midst of a burning furnace just like Zedekiah, and like Ahab whom the King of Babylon roasted in the fire Jer. 29:22.

This law did not move the children of God, Shadrach, Meshach and Abedinigo who were Jews. They were not afraid, nor dismayed, for they knew that the Lord their God is with them. Isa. 41:10.

They knew what God said that "They and you shalt have no other gods before Him", nor any graven image, like Nebuchadnezzar's golden image; that they shalt not bow down to them, nor serve them as the king commanded, for the Lord our God is a jealous God Exo. 20:1-5.

The jealous princes, as talebearers, ran to the King "Listen, O King, we seem to have three other kings apart from you". What? Where could such kings be? The princes said "they are right in your domain, they are the three Hebrews who refused to serve the image you set up". The princes were keen to get rid of the three whose honesty, integrity and steadfastness earned them the respect of the king, and in who the king had put his trust for good and wise counsel.

The king's anger was boiling, and rage was showing on his face. He asked them to be brought down saying "They shall surely not live if they bluntly refuse when I ask them why they have chosen to disobey my command".

Nebuchadnez-zar asked Shadrach., Meshach and Abednego if what he had heard was true, i.e. had they refused to bow to the beautifully decorated golden image he had set up. Their answer was sharp and unequivocal "Yes, live O King.

Where we came from, there we serve the True Living God by whom all things are made" Gen. 1:1, John 1:3. One thing we shall tell you is "For with our God, nothing is impossible" Lk. 1:37. "We were told by our fathers, Ah Lord God! Behold, thou hast made the heaven and the earth by thy great power and stretched out arm, and there is nothing too hard for this our God" Jer. 32:17.

The king could not believe what he was hearing, his heart was burning and he said in anger "remember that you are not in that land now, and by the look of things you are unlikely to go back". He said " you should realise that you are slaves here and you either bow to the image or face the burning furnace".

The trio said "We know our position, but the law of God, the one who is above all commanded us not to compromise with any graven image" Ex. 20:5, "For he hates images which he calls an abomination".

"Can that your Lord deliver you" Nebuchadnez-zar said. They answered "Yes, our God whom we serve is more than able to deliver us, O King. Haven't you heard that our God divided the Red Sea for our fathers, that he fed them forty years with manna, he made them drink water from the rock, he brought down the Walls of Jericho which fell down flat"?

The King's anger was burning higher as he thought "What an insult".

Before he spoke, Shadrach said, "Please King, let it be known to you that the people that do know their God shall do exploits just as God will reveal to you today. Dan 11:32(b).

They could read the King's state of mind as they said to him "Be it known to you dear king, that we shall not defy you in any other things". Just as the king thought that they were to compromise, Messach said "but as far as serving they gods, or worshipping thy golden image is concerned, we are forbidden to do it, this is just against our relationship with God".

He said "We abhor your gods, and while we like you personally as a king, we just will not serve what your hands have made".

The king asked another question "Are you willing to change your mind to bow down to the gods now or not?" Then Abednego burst out with rage that "Our God has commanded us not to be afraid of gods or golden images for they cannot do evil, neither also is it in them to do good" Jer. 10:5(b).

This saying let the cat out of the bag, the Bible says that Nebuchadnez-zar could not believe such boldness and defiance, for he could not know that our God says to us "Be bold, be strong, for the Lord our God is with us, anywhere, in any situation we may find ourselves" Josh. 1:9.

The form of his visage was changed against the three Hebrews that he commanded that they should heat the furnace one seven times. He commanded the most mighty men that were in his army to bind the three Hebrews and to cast them into the burning fiery furnace. The three Hebrews did not change their minds, they trusted the Word of God.

The King's anger backfired as the great intensity of the heat slew those men who bundled Shadrach and partners into the fire. The king and all spectators were sure that no one could ever survive such a burning furnace. To them, there was no hope. But Jesus Christ is above fire. He had said "Whenever we passeth through the waters, I will be with thee; and with the rivers, they shall not overflow thee; when thou walkest through the fire, thou shalt not be burned; neither shall the flame kindle upon thee Isa. 43:2.

As soon as they entered into the fire, Jesus Christ who is above all met them there and turned the fire to cool water, the air condition was perfect as they were loosed, walking inside the fire.

There and then, Jesus was discussing with the three Hebrews how the king's eyes alone would be opened to see that was going on. Nebuchadnez-zar stood up and shouted "Have we made a mistake? Have we made a mistake? Have we thrown four men into the fire? Though they thought the king was hung over from his wining of the previous day, they answered him "No".

The king insisted "I can see four men loose, walking majestically in the midst of the fiery furnace, and they have no hurt; the form of the fourth man is like the Son of God" Dan. 3:25.

What can He our God not do? His words are true and, as he said, "For I am the Lord thy God, the Holy One of Israel, thy Saviour. I gave Egypt for thy ransom Ethiopia and Se-ba for thee.

Since thou wast precious in my sight, thou hast been honourable, and I have loved thee therefore will I give men for thee, and people for thy life Isa. 43:3-4.

Then Nebuchadnez-zar went near the furnace, but was not burned. He had to testify of Jesus Christ the Son of God who is also above fire. He cried "Come out, and come hither, Servants of the most High God, come forth". Hallelujah. Then the three Hebrews came forth in the midst of the fire.

The princes, governors and company being gathered together saw these men, upon whose bodies the fire had no power, or was an hair of their head singed, neither were their coats changed, nor the smell of fire had passed on them. Hallelujah Dan. 3:1-29.

The same power that God possessed yesterday is still there today, and will remain for ever. For the owner is the same yesterday, the same today, and the same for ever Heb 13:8. He said "For I am the Lord, I change not, therefore ye Sons of Jacob (the three Hebrews) are not consumed by Nebuchadnez-zar's fire.

Malachi 3:6

Today, you may be in the fiery furnace of ill-health, Christ is ready to heal you by his stripes 1 Pet. 2:24, Exo. 15:26(b).

Are the enemies attacking you everywhere? Let it be known to you that victory will come from Christ, and will give you life, and that life more abundantly John 10:10.

Your fiery furnace may be unemployment. Christ is able to do more abundantly than you may ask, and God will supply all your needs according to his riches in glory by Christ Jesus Phil. 4:19.

Know fully well that I am talking about the Son of God who possesses all power in heaven and earth. He is Omnipotent, and possesses all power Job 37:16-24.

He is Omniscient i.e. He knows and sees all that concerns you John 1:45-50, John 13:11-17.

He is omnipresent: Just as you are reading this book, he sees you. If you ask him to teach you, he is willing to do so. Mt 18:18-20, Mt. 28:20.

He had power over the storm, including the Storm of your life. Once there arose a great storm of wind, and the waves beat into the ship so that it was now full.

And he was in the hinder part of the ship, asleep on a pillow; and they awoke him "Master, carest thou not that we perish"?

And he arose and rebuked the wind, and said unto the sea "Peace, be still, for the Prince of Peace commanded thee". And the wind ceased, and there was a great calm.

And he said unto them "Why are ye so fearful"? How is it that ye have no faith knowing that I who is above every situation am with thee?

And they feared exceedingly, and said one to another. "What manner of man is this that even the wind and the sea obey him? Mark 4:37-41.

He will quench the storm of your life, and everything will be still, and you shall know that surely Jesus Christ of Nazareth, Son of the Living God is truly above all. Amen.

AM I A CHRISTIAN

The followers of Christ were first called Christians in Antioch Acts 11:26. Today, many who are not Christians want to be associated with it, not knowing that the term was initially a derogatory term, because the disciples of Jesus set themselves apart, never conforming to the worldly way of doing things.

Christians set themselves apart, they were shewing all meekness and gentle characters. While the world is after physical riches, the Christians were after Spiritual riches, and growth; they never participated in fraudulent acts or robbery. They never violated government laws, or laws of God, they were going about their business in a proper and truthful way, knowing fully well that it is the blessing of God which maketh rich without adding sorrow to it Pro. 10:22.

The Christians were guided by the Holy Spirit, they and the world do things in parallel which cannot meet. They are washed in the Blood of Jesus Christ (who is above all) Rev. 7:14; and they have overcome the world as Jesus has done John 16:33. Knowing that they are ordained to eternal life Acts 13:48, they always rejoice in the Lord and are glad Phil. 4:4.

They know that they have an Everlasting Father who cannot fail them, even when they were persecuted, beaten, tossed hither and thither, thrown into the lions, tied to wheels of vehicles, yet they still continued to grow in numbers.

They were an amazing set of people whose goal was heaven. They believed the word of the Master that "In his father's house are many mansions, and he has gone to prepare a place for them" John 14:1-3. They had every cause to believe as they saw Christ who came from heaven, and went back to heaven. Their eyes were opened, and they knew that it was no fluke; but certainty ACTS 1:9-11. They believed his words that He is surely coming back. Nothing can change this because his words are true.

It is written that "So shall his word that goeth forth out of his mouth be". It shall not return unto him void, but it shall accomplish that which he pleases, and it shall prosper in the thing whereto he sent it Isa. 55:11. Truly, he will be coming back.

The Christians in Antioch remembered that He promised them that "He will send the Comforter, which is the Holy Spirit" John 14:16. As they remembered the day of Pentecost, when the Comforter did arrive Acts 2, they pressed forward continuing in the freshness of the Day of Pentecost when the Church of Jesus Christ of Nazareth was born, and the gates of hell shall not prevail against it Mt. 16:18.

No wonder that the Church is built upon the foundation of the apostles and prophets, Jesus Christ himself being the chief cornerstone Eph. 2:20.

The Christians in Antioch relied on what Christ said. They did one thing only, i.e. never mixed idol worship with serving God. They never compromised with other human religions, neither did they comply with any religion to inculcate them together. They knew too much about salvation than to go back into religion, knowing that, after they had escaped the pollution of the world through the knowledge of the Lord and Saviour Jesus Christ, they could not be tangled therein and have a latter end worse than the beginning.

For the Bible said "It had been better for them not to have known the way of righteousness than after they have known it, to turn from the holy commandment delivered unto them".

They know it happened unto the backsliders according to the proverb "The dog is turned to his own vomit again, and the sow that was washed to her wallowing in the mire 2 Peter 2:20-22". All these they kept in mind.

Christians were eager to let people see who Jesus Christ really is, i.e. that He is the Son of the Living God. They had not much money, therefore did not dole out money to convert people. Rather, they preached the Gospel that "God so loved the world that He gave his only begotten Son, that whosoever believeth in Him shall not perish, but have everlasting life John 3:16. That Christ is above all in his true perspective, that the people shall know the truth, and the truth shall set them free, that Christ being the Son shall indeed set them free from all their afflictions John 8:32-36. They always ended it up with the word "Only Jesus can save" Acts 4:12 Hallelujah.

Those that did not believe that only Jesus can save named the Believer's "Christians", i.e. people like Christ who are mere strangers on the earth Heb. 11:13, and whose home is heaven above. Amen.

NO CROSS – NO CROWN

There are different things that can be considered as a cross in a person's life. In fact, almost every success has a cross before the crown. In the natural, someone must follow the rule that stipulates that nothing ventured, nothing gained.

Someone has to work while he works, and play while he plays to be useful and happy. That is the way to obtain the crown. The key is that all that one does, it must be done with might because nothing can be achieved by halves.

In the natural, being awakened in the middle of the night by a baby is part of the cross for a parent. Staying up all night to swot for an examination and having to do a part time job with it is part of the Cross, which leads to the academic crown. Going to a place to preach the Gospel, and met with hostility and even beating is part of the Cross that leads to the Crown of a soul winner.

If, however, someone is not a Christian, and receives all things bad; it is not a cross leading to a crown but a punishment from Satan to his child. Fathers are entitled to rebuke their children.

Joseph carried a big cross, he was sold as a servant into Egypt. He held onto his dream knowing fully well that one day his brethren would bow down to him.

He got to Egypt where they hurt his feet with fetters. He was laid in iron; he counted it as part of the Cross to gain the crown. He spent time with criminals whose backgrounds were different from his. He knew that God was trying him as silver is tried Ps 66:10.

The king sent and loosed him, even the ruler of the people, and let him go free to become the Prime Minister in a foreign land. His crown included control of all the substance in the Foreign land, and to bind all the Princes at his pleasure, and taught all Egypt Senators wisdom, for he was controlled by God Almighty.

He brought his father and brothers who sold him into slavery to Egypt; and they became stronger than their hosts Ps. 105:17-24.

His cross was painful, but God's given crown is in history for ever.

The worst cross of all was borne by Jesus Christ. Right from infancy, Satan pursued him. His cross was to leave the place of his birth for a foreign land.

The Son of God, Jesus Christ of Nazareth grew up to start his mission. Satan knew that he could not win, and bribed him not to complete the work he came to do, so as to deprive him of the title "Saviour". The cross was painful torture beyond imagination.

Satan set up the Chief Priests, the Pharisees, and the Saducees against him. Jesus knew that all is part of the cross that would lead to the everlasting crown.

Jesus knew that he would be beaten, spat on, tortured, nailed to the cross with a crown of thorns befitting a sinner, and that he would die. Yet, Satan failed because the Son of God went through it all and resurrected from the grave on the third day, and spoilt Satan's party.

On that resurrection morning, the earth shook. The soldiers ran frightened and crying "Truly, truly, this is the Son of God" Hallelujah.

The Pharisees, Chief Priests and Saducees were told, and were afraid of the peoples' reaction. They tried all they could to suppress the news, but they failed.

Satan did everything to keep him on earth, but he failed. Now the Son of God with his crown is on his throne in heaven, and will one day judge every man that ever walked on the earth.

The work of salvation is completed and the Crown is in all power in earth, and heaven given to him Mt. 28:18.

The disciples were warned that there is cross on the way before their crowns and, truly all of them, expect John who was barred to the Island of Patmos, and Judas Iscariot who committed suicide for betraying Jesus Christ, were martyrs.

The disciples were not ignorant of what was at stake. That degradation, torture, beatings and death would come; but they believed Jesus, the Master, that everything he had said in the past would be as he said it would. They had their eyes set on the crowns, and not on the cross to come.

One day, there came a rich man who enjoyed, and could not part with his worldly crown. He kneeled down at Jesus feet, and asked him "Good Master, what shall I do that I may inherit eternal life"?

Jesus said to him "There is none good, but one. That is God. Thou knowest the commandments, just as many do know, but cannot keep them if that is what they rely on to save them."

Then he said "Do not commit adultery". If not in Jesus it is difficult.

"Do not kill" The rich man must have said "Thank God" he had never killed anyone. "Do not steal, neither bear false witness". The rich man would have said "Lord, I have never seen the four walls of a court to bear witness, whether false or true".

"Defraud not". He said "I don't, except selling at the usury. When Jesus said "honour thy father and mother", he would have said "Lord, I will fight anyone with all my money if he dishonours my father or mother, who I do honour greatly, Master, all these have I observed from my youth".

Jesus loved him for all the above, but then he dropped the bombshell "One thing thou lackest; go thy way, sell whatsoever thou hast, and give it to the poor, and thou shalt have treasure in heaven. Then come, take up thy cross and follow me" Mark 10:21.

The Bible says that the rich man was sad at that saying, and went away grieved; for he had great possession.

Christ went further to say that "It will be easier for a camel to go through the eye of a needle, than for a rich man to enter into the Kingdom of God". The cross was too much for the rich man. The disciples were greatly surprised beyond imagination, asking themselves "Who then can be saved"?

Jesus said "Worry not your hearts, there is a way, and you are there on the way". With men, it is impossible, but not with God, for God can widen the needle's hole, shrink the camel, and let the camel go through".

"So also will God save all that He has given to me, and will give them eternal life; for this is the Father's will, which hath sent me; that of all which he hath given me, I should lose nothing but should raise it up again at the last day. This is true of all of you with me, save Judas Iscariot".

"And this is the will of him that sent me, that every one which seeth the Son, and believeth on him, may have everlasting life; and I will raise him up at the last day" John 6:39-40. "This is their crown".

If the Lord himself gives such an assurance to us personally, then we should be prepared for all eventualities.

The disciples saw miracles unsurpassed by anyone. They saw Jesus' absolute honesty and believed all his sayings. When James and John, the sons of Zebedee asked to sit on the left and right hand of Jesus, he said to them "Ye know not what ye ask"; can you drink of the cup of death and torture that I drink of, and be baptised with the baptism of humiliation on the cross which will lead to the throne? Yet you will, but to sit on my right hand and on my left hand is not mine to give, but it shall be given to them for whom it is prepared.

There was a challenge, and every one of them worked harder to be on that throne, even:-

Stephen, who was the first Christian martyr had no fear to suffer man's torture, for he was a man full of faith and of the Holy Ghost. He lectured the Elders of Israel on who Jesus Christ is, and even prayed for forgiveness for those people, having seen where he would end up on the throne of God. He saw Jesus standing to welcome him home. What a great crown after being stoned.

Paul himself summed up his afflictions in 2 Cor. 11:23-33 as ,much labour with beatings with stripes above measure. He was in prison frequently, in need and in distress, in tumults, in labour, in watching and in fasting.

Thrice beating with rods. Five times he received forty stripes save one. He was once stoned, thrice he suffered ship-wreck and he was often in perils of waters, robbers, and Jews and Gentiles, in perils in the city, in perils in the wilderness, in perils in the sea, in perils among false brethren. Those who say that they were Christians, but were only in mouth and lips, but their hearts were far away from the Lord Mt. 15:8.

He went through in weariness and pain in watching, often in hunger and thirst and fasting often, in cold and in nakedness.

In Damascus, the governor under A-re-tas the King kept the city of Damascus with a garrison, desirous to apprehend him. Through a window in a basket was he let down by the wall, and escaped his hands Acts 9:25.

It was all like a game of cat and mouse for all the disciples, just as the people hated Jesus, so also did they hate the disciples.

Paul was ready to leave the world with an assurance that "heaven is his home".

He boldly said "For I am now ready to be martyred, and the time of my departure is at hand".

I have fought a good fight, I have finished my course, I have kept the faith; Henceforth, there is laid up for me a crown of righteousness, which the Lord, the righteous Judge shall give me at that day; and not to me only, but unto all them also that love his appearing. He knew what awaited him in heaven.

He was beheaded in Rome by Emperor Nero around A.D. 68.

Peter, meaning "Rock", who behaved according to his name. He was the only disciple that followed Jesus after his arrest, even though it was from afar off.

He was reputed to have told his executioners not to crucify him as his Lord, but to do it head downward, to show that he bowed to Jesus Christ as Lord and Saviour. Peter was crucified around A.D. 68 just like PAUL ON June 29th, their feast day.

Andrew, Brother of Peter. He too was crucified on an X shaped cross at Achaia by the Roman Governor Aegus on Feast day, November 30th A.D. 60.

James, Son of Zebedee was the elder brother of John the Evangelist. He perished by the sword under Herod Agrippa on Feast day, July 25th 44A.D.

John, the Evangelist, brother of James was reputed to have been plunged into a cauldron of boiling oil. He escaped unhurt, and died a natural death at Ephesus around AD 97.

Jude or Thaddeus, brother of James, the less reputedly martyred in Persia. He was tied to a running chariot on their Feast Day, October 28th AD 67.

Matthew (Zaccheus) was a Galilean, Son of Alphaeus, originally known as Levi. He was a publican and a Tax Collector, and was called to apostleship by the Lord. He was reputed to have been the first to write the Gospel after our Lord's ascension.

Matthew, like the others, was martyred by the sword in Ethiopia on Feast day, September 21st.

Philip was one of the seven appointed Deacons. He was a native of Bethsaida, zealous for the work of Christ. He was said to have been hanged against pillars in Phrigia on the feast day.

James the Less, the Son of Alphaeus, and Mary of Cleopas who was the sister of the Blessed Virgin Mary.. He was stoned by the Jews, and then killed with a fuller's club on feast day May 1st AD. 62.

Thomas. All the doubts went out of him, having seen the resurrected Jesus Christ. He went as far as India to proclaim Jesus, that He is the Son of God, that he came from above and is above all. The Thomas Christians of India traced their origin to him. Thomas, like the others, was run through with a lance at Coromanda on Feast Day December 21st.

Bartholomew, one of the twelve apostles of Christ said also like Thomas to have preached the gospel in India. He was skinned alive in Armenia Feast day, August 24th.

Simon was said to have been crucified in Percia on Feast Day, October 28th.

Today, many people say that salvation is free. We must all look at the great price paid by the Lord Jesus Christ, the apostles, and the disciples.

Let us remember how they were killed, not allowed to sleep in peace, but violently killed. They all carried their cross with dignity and are all now at Christ's bosom.

Let us all preach that Christ is the Son of God who died for our sins. It may bring thorns and thistles here on earth, but surely a crown from the Lord Jesus is waiting for us to wear.

Christ Jesus said "And behold, I come quickly; and my reward is with me, to give every man according as his work shall be".

"I am the Alpha and Omega, the beginning and the end. The first and the last. Blessed are they that do his commandments, that they may have a right to the tree of life, and may enter in through his gates into the city" Rev 22: 12-14.

MY PERSONAL TESTIMONIES

Have you ever repeatedly searched a pocket in your room and then found some money in it on the third search?

No one has what he does not possess, but there is a Provider, Jesus Christ is his name. I had been hearing the phrase "Supernatural provision", but I was not quite sure about it until it happened to me.

I had four children, in higher institutions and secondary school and my monthly expenses were about £480. Once, I had only a day left before all these expenses became due, and I had only £7 in my pocket.

As usual, I prayed and gave praises to God, then I went out.

As I walked 200 yards from my house, I met my brother-in-law at a junction in his car. He asked me "Why are you not in your car"? I told him that my car needed repairs. He asked me if I needed his mechanic to come and repair it, then God put it in his hearth top give me £500. Praise God!

I turned back to my house, and began praising God, saying:-

I am singing unto the Lord, singing Hallelujah
I am dancing unto the Lord, dancing Hallelujah
I am jumping unto the Lord, jumping Hallelujah
I am clapping unto the Lord, clapping Hallelujah

An hour or so later, a cousin buzzed at my door. I heartily welcomed him in with confidence, knowing that I could confidently buy him a drink without needing to worry about my children's money.

He said "my brother, I can't stay long but I just came to drop this by". He handed me an envelope and left. Inside the envelope was £250.

From £7 to £757 within two hours. I could not read the Bible as normal. I ran around the house singing:-

What a mighty God I serve (2ce.)
Heaven and Earth adore Him
Angels bow before Him
What a mighty God I serve

God hadn't finished his miracles yet. About 6pm that day, my mother-in-law came by with provisions, and she gave us £200. £950 came my way without me spending a penny.

"The blessings of the Lord maketh rich without adding any sorrow unto it" Pro. 10:22. I went to the adjacent room to thank God. People down the street could hear my praises to God.

This proves that, beyond reasonable doubt, "With God, all things are possible" Lk. 1:37. It also proves that "God supplies all his children's needs according to His riches in glory by Christ Jesus" Phil, 4:19.

MY PHYSICAL NEED IS MET

The fact is that God said that "I am the God that healeth thee" Exo. 15:26, and this should not be taken as a joke by anyone who trusts in the Lord Jesus Christ.

Before I accepted Jesus Christ as my Lord and personal Saviour, I was bedevilled by chronic asthma. Thank God I didn't die because I definitely wouldn't have gone to heaven.

The doctor was being called out at least three times a week, and the asthma seemed totally resistant to drugs.

However, the asthma finally got blown away by the stripes of Jesus Christ 1 Peter 2:24. For the past fifteen years, I have been asthma free. The doctor enquired of me from my wife, and I told her "I have joined Christ's Supernatural World Health Service" The blood of Jesus has been my injections, and the stripes that Jesus received have been the instruments for my healing.

There were thirty-nine stripes laid on the back of Jesus, and no one has thirty nine diseases. Surely, one of Christ's stripes is capable of healing you.

Again, whilst working as a Bank Manager, I needed glasses to read, but now I read the faintest letters in the newspapers without glasses.

One morning, my car was being washed under my watchful eye. While I was asking the driver questions, I put my glasses on the carburettor, under the open bonnet. Suddenly, the driver closed the bonnet and my glasses said bye-bye.

I went upstairs and tried to read something which was quite blurred, to say the least. I was due to get another but it was weekend so I went to church on Sunday where I found I was able to read the Bible quite clearly.

Fifteen years later, I still haven't gone in for replacement glasses. What a physician Christ is! He is the greatest Physician.

He is Christ the Sympathiser.

I am sure you have read how God showed his sympathy on me, calling me with his great hand, anointing me with the Holy Ghost and power. He can do the same for you. He is calling you, "Come unto me" is his word to you today.

DO YOU BELIEVE IN GOD'S PROTECTION OR NOT?

I'd like you to read what happened to me.

My wife had a dream that a thief entered our house. She was praying so fervently in the middle of the night that I had to join her in prayer, that the Lord would protect us from Robbers. The morning had hardly dawned when I bought extra chains to lock the doors and keep the thieves outside.

As it transpired, it was not the thief of this world but the devil who was about to try to steal a life from the family.

One of our children was coming to London, and we had to travel to Lagos to buy him travellers cheques. As we set out on public transport, we pleaded with a woman to allow my son to sit in front to allow room for his long legs.

When we got to Lagos, we were told to return the following week so we left the money, and set out on our return journey.

When we were coming, a tall man sat in the front so there was no one to swap places with my son who sat at the back of the car.

About six kilometres to our destination, the front rim and tyre of the vehicle came off whilst we were travelling at speeds of around 120km per hour. The man who sat where my son would have sat died instantly. Meanwhile, my son's passport had dropped almost 200 yards away and someone brought it up to me.

To God's glory, we did not lose my son's life, nor the money we took with us. Praise God, the Great Protector.

I thank the Lord who by all these things, made me realise that the Bible is true, and that Christ, as He said, is above ALL things. He is a Saviour, protector and a provider.

He will not leave us, nor forsake us. He is a present help in times of our needs.